Chief Justice Profiles

CHIEF JUSTICE PROFILES

OUR HIDDEN LEADERS

Philip Secor

iUniverse LLC
Bloomington

CHIEF JUSTICE PROFILES
OUR HIDDEN LEADERS

iUniverse books may be ordered through booksellers or by contacting:

iUniverse
1663 Liberty Drive
Bloomington, IN 47403
www.iuniverse.com
1-800-Authors (1-800-288-4677)

Because of the dynamic nature of the Internet, any web addresses or links contained in this book may have changed since publication and may no longer be valid. The views expressed in this work are solely those of the author and do not necessarily reflect the views of the publisher, and the publisher hereby disclaims any responsibility for them.

Any people depicted in stock imagery provided by Thinkstock are models, and such images are being used for illustrative purposes only.

Certain stock imagery © Thinkstock.

ISBN: 978-1-4917-0760-9 (sc)
ISBN: 978-1-4917-0792-0 (e)

Library of Congress Control Number: 2013916537

Printed in the United States of America.

iUniverse rev. date: 9/6/2013

TABLE OF CONTENTS

PREFACE

CHIEF JUSTICES OF THE United States Supreme Court are among the most powerful political figures in American history. They and their colleagues on the High Court have the constitutional authority to uphold or strike down many of the most important decisions of the president, congress and state and local governments. They are not elected by the public but appointed by the president and, once appointed, they serve for life. To all intents and purposes they are responsible to no one but themselves.

Despite this enormous power, the seventeen men who have presided over the Supreme Court since the founding of the Republic have received little attention from American historians. Most of them are unknown by the general public. To test the accuracy of this generalization, I recently interviewed fifty people, many with college educations. They could, on average, name only five of the Chief Justices and fewer than half even knew the name of the current Chief Justice, the honorable John Roberts.

As a longtime student, teacher and writer in the field of American government, I have been amazed that so little attention has been paid to the Chief Justices. How could the wielders of such enormous influence been of so little interest both to scholars and the American people generally?

To answer this question is one purpose of this book. My major goal, however, is to remedy the problem by providing biographical portraits of each of the Chief Justices so that the general reader may have readily at hand a useable source of information about some of the most important and influential figures in our history and be awakened to a continuing interest in this highly important position of Chief Justice of the Supreme Court.

CHIEF JUSTICES BY LENGTH OF SERVICE AND PRESIDENTS

CHIEF JUSTICE	YEARS	DATES	PRESIDENT(S) IN OFFICE
John Marshall	34	1801-1835	Jefferson, Madison, Monroe, John Quincy Adams, Jackson.
Roger Taney	28	1836-1864	Jackson, Van Buren, Harrison. Tyler, Polk, Taylor, Pierce, Buchanan, Lincoln.
Melville Fuller	22	1888-1910	Cleveland, B. Harrison, McKinley, T. Roosevelt, Taft.
William Rehnquist	19	1986-2005	Reagan, G. Bush, Clinton, G. W. Bush.
Warren Burger	17	1969-1986	Nixon, Ford, Carter, Reagan.
Earl Warren	16	1953-1969	Eisenhower, Kennedy, L. Johnson.
Morrison Waite	14	1974-1988	Grant, Hayes, Garfield, Arthur.
Edward White	11	1910-1921	Taft, Wilson
Charles Evans Hughes	11	1930-1941	Hoover, Franklin Roosevelt.
William Howard Taft	9	1921-1930	Harding, Coolidge, Hoover.
Salmon Chase	9	1964-1973	Lincoln, A. Johnson, Grant.
JOHN ROBERTS	8	2005-	G. W. Bush, Obama.
Fred Vinson	7	1946-1953	Truman.
John Jay	6	1789-1795	Washington.
Harlan Fiske Stone	5	1941-1946	Franklin Roosevelt, Truman.
Oliver Ellsworth	4	1796-1800	Washington, John Adams.
John Rutledge	1/2	1795	Washington

John Jay

JOHN JAY
(1745-1828)
1790-1794

I

PROBABLY NOT ONE IN a thousand Americans today could name the first three chief justices of the U. S. Supreme Court. Yet, in their own day each of these men was one of the most famous and important persons in the country and seriously considered for the presidency of the new nation. All three played active leadership roles during the Revolution, were involved in the creation of the new government and served variously as members of the Constitutional Convention, and the First and Second Continental Congresses, authors of *The Federalist Papers,* and governors of their states.

None of the three was more important in the life of the new nation than our first Chief Justice, John Jay, who came from two prominent New York families which had been highly successful merchants and powerful political figures in New York City for several generations before his birth in 1745. One grandfather, on his mother's side, was a Van Courtland who had served in the New York General Assembly and was twice mayor of New York City (New Amsterdam). His paternal grandfather had come to the New York area from France and soon became very wealthy trading in many products produced in the new country, including animal furs, timber and wheat. Jay's father inherited this great wealth and passed it on to John, who, consequently, had both the wealth and the leisure to pursue a career in the law and in public service.

What makes John Jay unique among all chief justices is that he was the first and therefore set many lasting precedents for the nature and power of the position. He was in other respects, as well, a "founding father" of the new nation: a member of the First and Continental Congresses, a delegate at the Constitutional Convention and author of many of the key provisions in that founding document, one of the authors of the *Federalist Papers,* a drafter of the *Declaration of Independence* and the first ambassador to such important countries as England and Spain.

II

Jay grew up just north of New York City, in Rye on December 12, 1745. The Jay family was prominent among the leading merchant families in New York. John's paternal grandfather grand-father had fled from France in the seventeenth century when the Roman Catholic Church was persecuting Protestants. His maternal grandfather was a Van Courtland who, as previously noted, had served as mayor of New York City (New Amsterdam) in the earliest years of the colonial settlement.

As a small boy, John was educated by private tutors. When the family moved to nearby New Rochelle in 1753, he studied under an Anglican priest before entering Kings College (Columbia University), graduating in 1764. After spending a number of years as a law clerk in the City, he was admitted to the bar and opened his own practice in 1771.

As war with Britain approached in 1774, John married Sarah ("Sally") Livingston who was very active in the movement for American independence—and therefore, war with England. She was a woman of notable charm and beauty—a style-setter in women's fashion and a high-spirited, popular hostess. Not surprisingly, she had a major influence on John's public career, travelling with him everywhere including his service abroad as an ambassador. The couple had six children and lived in a fine house in Katonah, New York which is now a National Historic Landmark.

Jay was a life-long Episcopalian, serving in many important church positions including senior warden of the prestigious Trinity Church in New York City. As such he was a member of a tolerant church characterized by its commitment to the *via media*—a broad "middle way" which welcomed a wide variety of beliefs and distained religious and political certainty (absolutism). No doubt the leadership in the church disapproved many of the doctrinaire opinions which came to characterize the career of this highly distinguished member of their flock. Forexample, there were his efforts to prevent Roman Catholics from holding public office and his insistence that only Christians—excepting Roman Catholics, of course—should be elected to public office. In 1816, he wrote: "Providence has given to our people the choice of their leaders and it is the duty . . . of our Christian nation to select and prefer Christians for their rulers."

III

On the very day that George Washington signed the law creating the Supreme Court—September 24, 1789—he appointed John Jay as the first Chief Justice. As did many of his successors, Jay intensely disliked the office and behaved accordingly. The historian, Leo Pfeifer, has described him in this role as "very undistinguished."

When the Supreme Court held its first session, on February 1, 1790, only Jay and two other Justices appeared. In any event, there was no business to perform. The court did not meet again for six months. In fact, not for almost three years were there any cases to decide. The justices, however, did have a few other duties to perform including service as circuit court judges in the three judicial districts in the country at the time.

Jay hated all this running about the country and soon ran for governor of New York while still a member of the high court. He lost that election to George Clinton. Another assignment he accepted while on the Court was that of Special Ambassador to England to negotiate the settlement of a number of disagreements, including the boarding of American ships at sea in order to "impress" American sailors into the British navy. During his year in England on this assignment, Jay had virtually no success at all. For this failure he was widely branded at home as a "Tory" and sometimes even as a "traitor."

In 1795, Jay ran again for governor of New York. This time he won the election and served in that office until 1801. Meantime, he had run for the presidency in both 1796 and 1800, losing respectively to John Adams and Thomas Jefferson.

During Jay's service as Chief Justice, only one really significant case was decided—*Chisholm v. Georgia,* in 1793. This case involved the confiscation by the state of Georgia of land which had been owned by British sympathizers. Chisholm, one Tories involved, sued the state for restoration of the land. Georgia responded that a sovereign state could not be sued, arguing, therefore, that the Supreme Court had no jurisdiction in the case. The argument was sound. The Constitution itself probably would never have been ratified by the states if such a right been included in the founding document. Also, in *Federalist Paper 81,* Alexander Hamilton had called the very idea "absurd." However, Article 111, Section 2 of the Constitution does say that the Supreme Court shall have jurisdiction in any case involving conflict between states and citizens.

John Jay and his colleagues on the court decided the case in Chisholm's favor. The reaction was swift and emphatic. Georgia officials declared they would never obey the court ruling. In the event, no serious effort was ever made to collect the money allegedly owed to Chisholm and so the matter ended.

Shortly after the Chisholm decision, the Eleventh Amendment to the Constitution was approved allowing the Supreme Court jurisdiction in any lawsuit between a State and a citizen of the U.S. Jay was widely accused of being pro-British because the decision, if enforced, would have benefited Tories at the expense of states and virtually bankrupted many states. All over the country Jay was burned in effigy.

IV

John Jay left the court in 1795 to be governor of New York State and ran for president in 1796 against John Adams and again in 1800 against Thomas Jefferson. He lost both elections by large margins. In 1801, he left public life altogether and retired to his home in Westchester County, New York. Here he lived peaceably, quietly worked as a farmer and enjoyed good health for some twenty-eight years.

His main interests in retirement were agricultural experimentation to improve both the quantity and quality of a number of farm products and an active role in the Protestant Church, especially his own Episcopal Church. He was particularly active in creating non-denominational groups to promote Bible study and to encourage young men to enter the ministry.

In these later years, Jay modified a number of his earlier views, most notably on the issue of slavery which he came gradually to oppose in principle almost as much as he had once supported it as a practical necessity to save the Union.

Most historians have praised Jay's career in public service. Irving Dilliard, for example, in a chapter in Volume I of Friedman and Israel's *The Justices of the U.S. Supreme Court* (1969), has written:

> To the end [of his life], prudence, compassion, gratitude and fairness have marked the career of John Jay. Above all, fairness ruled his life for, as far back as the Revolution, he could be fair even to England . . ." when he wrote: "The destruction of Old England would hurt me. I wish it well; it afforded my ancestors an asylum from persecution.

In May, 1829, Jay died of palsy at his home in Bedford, New York. He was eighty-four years old. There are many memorials to his life and career, including cities in New York and Vermont, the John Jay College of Criminal Justice at the City College of New York and the John Jay Scholarship at Columbia University. Mountain peaks in Alaska and Vermont are also named in his honor.

John Rutledge

JOHN RUTLEDGE
(1739-1800)
July-December, 1795

I

THE SECOND CHIEF JUSTICE, John Rutledge, was in many ways a copy of his predecessor. His role as a "founding father" who served in the Second Continental Congress, as a delegate to the Constitutional Convention and as an opponent of "democracy" as too radical a form of government all echo the ideas and policies of John Jay. What was radically different was his very short term as Chief Justice which meant that he would have virtually no influence on the court's development, unlike Jay who served for six years and, as we have seen, had a significant impact on the future of the high court.

II

John Rutledge was born and raised in Charleston, South Carolina. Following his birth in 1739, he was educated at home by his father and a local Anglican minister. His father, John, was a physician who had immigrated from Scotland. John had six siblings, all younger than he. After studying law for a time at home, he traveled to England where he studied at London's Middle Temple. When he returned home to

Charleston, he opened his practice and before long was a successfully attorney known throughout that part of the country.

In 1763, Rutledge married Elizabeth Grimke. They had ten children and, by all accounts, a loving relationship. When Elizabeth died thirty years later, John was devastated. He never married again.

III

A member of the anti-British Stamp Act Congress of 1765, Rutledge was one of the most influential opponents of "taxation without representation"—a battlecry of the Revolutionary War and a signal feature of the American colonial government. Between 1794 and 1798, he served in the First and Second Continental Congresses.

As war with England approached, Rutledge was elected President (Governor) of South Carolina and was instrumental in preparing military fortifications, especially on Sullivan's island in Charles Harbor. When the British attacked this fort in 1776, they suffered one of their worst defeats in the war.

In 1778, while still governor of South Carolina, Rutledge vetoed a new constitution developed by the legislature. He asserted that it went too far toward creating a "direct democracy" which was tantamount to anarchy. When the legislature overrode his veto, he resigned the governorship. A year later, he was elected to that post again as the British army was in the process of taking over most of the state.

After the war, in 1787, Rutledge was chosen by the state legislature to represent South Carolina at the Constitutional Convention in Philadelphia. He was very creative and largely successful at the Convention, especially as chair of the Committee on Detail. Noteworthy are his successes in assuring a single executive chief for the new nation and a major role for the Senate in drafting legislation.

Among Rutledge's less successful efforts at the Convention was his advocacy of allowing slavery in the entire country. If this was not done, he argued, Southern states would never become part of a new "United" States.

IV

In 1789, Rutledge became a justice on the first Supreme Court. About two years later, he resigned this post, there having been no cases to decide. Then, in 1795, when John Jay resigned as Chief Justice, Washington appointed Rutledge as an interim replacement while the Senate was not in session. Almost at once, the new Chief Justice made a public statement which was strongly critical of his predecessor for his work while arranging a treaty with England that had ended the Revolutionary War. In this speech he said that Jay and the Senate "were fools and knaves duped by British sophistry or bribed by British gold." Not surprisingly, these remarks angered Washington and many members of the Senate. When Senate approval was sought to make his interim appointment on the Court official, that body said, "NO!"

There were only two cases of any lasting significance during Rutledge's short term on the High Court. These were *United States v. Peters* which ruled that Federal District Courts have no jurisdiction in crimes against Americans in international waters and *Talbert v. Johnson* which ruled that an American does not lose his citizenship by becoming a citizen of another country or by renouncing his citizenship in an American state. Multiple citizenship is constitutional.

V

For much of Rutledge's later life he was afflicted with mental disorders which often resulted in bizarre public behavior that damaged his reputation. As early as 1795, when he received his commission as Chief Justice, he was, according to a leading historian of that period, "quite likely already insane." This may well have been caused by the Senate's rejection of Washington's nomination of him as Chief Justice. He was also greatly embarrassed by the aforementioned negative reactions to Washington's attacks of Jay over the peace treaty with England.

Shortly after he finally withdrew from public service in 1796, it was widely reported that he had tried and nearly succeeded to drown himself. Nevertheless, he lived for another four years, dying at home in Charleston on July 23, 1800. He was only sixty years old.

Oliver Ellsworth

OLIVER ELLSWORTH
(1745-1807)
1796-1780

I

THE THIRD OF THE "founding father"- chief justices was, like his two predecessors, actively engaged in the most important developments shaping the politics and government of the new nation.

Oliver Ellsworth was an excellent student and scholar, was happily married and held important posts in state government. He also played a key role at the Constitutional Convention, as an ambassador. While on the Supreme Court, he was involved in a number of decisions which would to define the very nature of the American federal system of government.

II

Born in Windsor, Connecticut in 1745, Ellsworth studied at Yale, completing his college work at Princeton with Phi Beta Kappa honors. After studying law on his own, he passed the Connecticut bar exam and was soon one of the most successful and well-regarded attorneys in the Northeast.

In 1772, Oliver married Abigail Wolcott, a member of a prominent Connecticut family. The couple had nine children and an apparently loving and mutually supportive marriage.

III

Shortly after marriage, during the early years of the Revolutionary War, Ellsworth was elected one of Connecticut's representatives to the First Continental Congress. During the War, he also served as a judge on a number of state courts. By 1784, had begun a four-year term on the Connecticut Supreme Court. While still on that court, he was selected as a delegate to the U.S. Constitutional Convention in Philadelphia. Thus began one of the most important parts of his entire career in public life, playing a major role in the formation of our founding document as an independent nation.

Shortly after his work at the Convention, Ellsworth was elected as one of the first two senators from Connecticut. Serving in the Senate from 1789-1796, he was highly respected and admired as one of the leaders in that new legislative body. President John Adams went so far as to call him President Washington's "firmest pillar" in the Senate.

As a Senator, Ellsworth continued to fix his attention on the Supreme Court. He played a major role in writing the *Judiciary Act* of 1789–the first law passed in the Senate. He was personally responsible for several parts of that formative legislation, including Section 25 which gave the high court power to overrule state court decisions that upheld state laws viewed by the Supreme Court to be contrary to the U. S. Constitution. He also played a key role in the senate's approval of the Bill of Rights addition to the constitution. And, if all of this were not enough, he was involved in creating the first Bank of the United States and in plans to fund the growing national debt.

And, oh yes, one must not forget that this incredible man found time to run for the presidency against John Adams in 1796, but winning only eleven electoral vote in that contest.

IV

Ellsworth was selected by President Washington to serve as Chief Justice of the Supreme Court in 1796. He served for only about four years, leaving because of ill health in 1800. While Chief Justice, he was involved in deciding and writing opinions in a number of decisions which were to set lasting precedents defining the power of the high court and the very nature of the federal system of government.

The first of these cases was *Hylton v. United States* (1798) which declared that any state law which was, in the court's opinion, in conflict with a U. S. treaty with a foreign country was unconstitutional. The rationale given was that treaties are laws of the federal government and, like all such laws, take precedence over state laws.

Another leading case, *Hollingsworth v. Virginia* (1798), severely limited the president's power *viz a viz* that of the high court. Here, Ellsworth and his colleagues argued that the president has no role whatsoever in the process of amending the U. S. Constitution.

Calder v. Bull (1798) is probably Ellsworth's most memorable decision on the Court. In this case, the court ruled that any state law which was, in its view, contrary to the Constitution was *ipso facto* invalid. No other Supreme Court decision had so emphatically and definitively diminished the power of state governments at a time when the national government was in its infancy and state law dominated the legal landscape. Simultaneously, this decision definitively extended the power of the high court.

In other cases, like *New York v. Connecticut* (1798), the Ellsworth court further expanded the authority of the Supreme Court. In this case it ruled that in cases where the laws of two states were in conflict, the Supreme Court would have original and total jurisdiction.

V

Oliver Ellsworth was one of the few Chief Justices who did not live for at least a few years after leaving office. He served briefly on the

Connecticut Governor's Council after leaving the court in 1800 but soon became seriously ill, possibly due to his earlier travels in France.

He died at home in 1807. There are not many memorials to him. The only notable one is the town of Ellsworth, Maine.

John Marshall

JOHN MARSHALL
(1755-1835)
1801-1835

I

THE THIRD CHIEF JUSTICE is, perhaps, the most important in American history. Not surprisingly, his name, if not his life's work, is the best remembered of all who have held that office. He is, without doubt, the man who elevated the Supreme Court to the position of co-equal with the president and Congress in the federal government. He is the longest serving of all chief justices, holding that post for thirty-four years, from 1801 to 1835 and serving during the presidencies of no less than six men: Thomas Jefferson, James Madison, James Monroe, John Quincy Adams and Andrew Jackson.

Marshall was one of the leading Federalist Party members of his day. In the face of the strong states'-rights policies of the dominant Democratic/Republican Party, he was an advocate of a strong national government which he viewed as necessary if the new country was to be successful in its economic and political development and in its place among the nations of the world.

II

John Marshall was born in a log cabin on the Virginia frontier on September 24, 1755—the first of fifteen children. His father. Thomas, was a successful land surveyor for Lord Fairfax who was the British governor of the territory. The two men became close friends and Fairfax was, before long, the patron of young John, welcoming the boy into his home to use his library as part of his early education which was closely supervised by his father. (There were, as yet, no schools in this remote area.)

During the Revolutionary War, John became a close friend of George Washington, serving with him at Valley Forge. After the war, he studied law under the famous George Wythe who was Chancellor at William and Mary College in Williamsburg. Here he was an outstanding student, earning Phi Beta Kappa honors. In 1788, he was admitted to the Virginia bar and opened what would soon be a successful practice with clients throughout the state.

III

In 1782, Marshall began his career in politics when he was elected to the Virginia House of Delegates where he was to serve from 1782-1789 and 1795-1796. While a member of the state legislature in 1788, he was selected by that body as a delegate from Virginia to the U. S. Constitutional Convention meeting in Philadelphia. Here he worked closely with James Madison and Edmond Randolph for ratification of the Constitution. Their principal opponent was the fire-brand individualist revolutionary, Patrick Henry of "give me liberty or give me death" fame who opposed any move toward a strong national government.

President Washington offered Marshall the position of U. S. Attorney General in 1795 and he declined. But, in 1796 he accepted President Adams' appointment as one of three "ministers" to France charged with resolving conflicts with that country. Because of what was widely perceived as his success in this mission, he began to gain a national reputation. In 1799, he decided to run for Congress and won the election despite the fact that he was a Federalist and his congressional district was predominantly Democratic/Republican.

Scarcely had John begun his term in Congress when President John Adams appointed him to his cabinet as Secretary of State. In this position, he served for only about a year—long enough for him to negotiate the final peace treaty with France.

IV

In the presidential election of 1800, Thomas Jefferson prevailed and the Federalists were finally out of power in Washington. This should have doomed any hope Marshall might have had for high office. But something most unusual happened which would elevate him to one of the highest offices in the country—Chief Justice of the Supreme Court. It happened in this way:

On the night before newly elected president, Thomas Jefferson, took office, the lame-duck president, John Adams, and his Federalist Congress passed a law altering the size of the Supreme Court in such a way as to thwart Jefferson's plan to "pack" the court with his own justices. Another part of Adam's plan was to select a strongly Federalist chief justice who would be against the incoming president's policies. John Marshall was his choice. This entire episode has since been known as the "midnight judges act."

Roger Brooke Taney

ROGER BROOKE TANEY
(1777-1864)
1936-1964

I

THE FIFTH CHIEF JUSTICE, Roger Brooke Taney, was the second longest-serving, with twenty-eight years in office. Combined with his immediate predecessor, John Marshall, who had held the post for thirty-four years, these two men served for a total of sixty-two consecutive years during a very formative period in American history.

Among a number of important Supreme Court decisions while Taney was Chief Justice, his fame rests primarily on one case: *Dred Scott v. Sanford*. In this case, the court held that Black people living in the United States were not citizens of the country.

Taney is also memorable for being a staunch supporter of states' rights in a time of growing national power and for being the first Roman Catholic to serve as Chief Justice.

II

Roger Taney was born in Calvert County, Maryland, the second of seven children growing up on a prosperous tobacco plantation. He received his early education from tutors and then entered Dickinson College in Pennsylvania, graduating with honors in 1795. He read law for a time and then passed the Maryland bar exam in 1799. Before long, he was prospering in his practice and well-known throughout the area.

In 1806, the young attorney married Anne Key. The couple apparently enjoyed a happy life together and had six children. Anne died 1845, some twenty years before Roger's death.

III

In 1799, the same year in which he began his career as an attorney, Taney ran successfully for the Maryland State Senate as a Federalist. He was re-elected in 1816, this time on the Democratic ticket after the Federalist Party had ceased to exist. Some years later, in 1824, he was an active supporter of Andrew Jackson in Jackson's unsuccessful bid for the presidency against John Quincy Adams. When Jackson was elected in 1828, he rewarded his staunch supporter by appointing him Attorney General of the United States. In that office, Taney was a strong advocate of slavery in whatever states allowed it. In 1833, Jackson nominated Roger to his Cabinet as Secretary of Treasury, a position he had held as an interim appointment for several months. When the Senate rejected the nomination, Taney returned to his law practice in Maryland.

IV

President Jackson brought his good friend, Roger, back into public life in a dramatic way in 1836. He submitted his name to the Senate for appointment as Chief Justice of the Supreme Court to replace John Marshall who had died the previous year. In what would become a controversial response to the nomination, the Senate followed the lead of several of its most powerful members who vigorously opposed the nomination—John C. Calhoun, Henry Clay and Daniel Webster. After a lengthy and nasty debate, Taney was approved and became

Chief Justice, a position he would hold for twenty-eight years, longer than any other person except his predecessor, John Marshal, who, as noted earlier, had held that position for thirty-four years.

As Chief Justice, Taney was an avid supporter of states' rights in the face of the growing power of the national government. In one of his most important decisions of the Court, *Mayor of the City of New York v. Miln* (1837), he held that the state government could make requirements on shipping entering the Port of New York despite Congressional power to regulate the same under the "commerce clause" of the Constitution.

Another of Taney's consistent positions on the Court was his opposition the rights of Blacks when these rights were denied by states. In *Prigg v. Pennsylvania* (1842), for example, his Court upheld a state law that prohibited the enforcement of any other laws interfering with the state's power to limit the rights of Blacks.

By far the most famous (infamous?) of Taney's decisions was *Dred Scott v. Sanford* (1857), a decision which many believe led eventually to the Civil War. (This idea was bases on the assumption that if southern states had been allowed to keep slavery, they would not have seceded and war would have been avoided.) In the case, the Court held that Congress had no authority to halt the spread of slavery in the states or the new territories and that any attempt to do so, including the "Missouri Compromise" of 1820, would be unconstitutional.

Among those who were severely critical of the *Dred Scott* decision, was President Lincoln. Notwithstanding such important opposition, Taney defended his decision largely on the grounds that African Americans had been excluded from citizenship from the earliest days of the new Republic because of the basic inferiority of that race. In the decisions itself, he had written:

> It is difficult at this day to realize the state of public opinion in regard to the unfortunate race which prevailed at the time of the Declaration of Independence and when the Constitution of the United States was framed and adopted; but the public history of every European nation displays it in a manner too

plain to be mistaken. They had for more than a century before been regarded as being of an inferior order, and altogether unfit to associate with the white race, either in social or political relations, and so far unfit that they had no rights which the white man was bound to respect.

Further evidence—if any is needed—of Taney's complete split with President Lincoln came a few years later in the case of *Ex parte Merryman* (1861) in which the Taney court ruled that Lincoln's Congress had no right to issue a writ of *habeas corpus* anywhere in the country because the Constitution did not expressly grant such a right. Lincoln was appalled at the decision and responded by ignoring it and executing the writ anyway.

V

Not long after the *Merryman* decision, Taney became seriously ill. He died in October, 1864 at the age of eighty-seven.

Among surprisingly few memorials to this influential and long-serving Chief Justice are a county in Missouri, a street in Baltimore, a statue at the Maryland State House and a statue in Washington D. C..

Salmon Chase

SALMON P. CHASE
(1808-1873)
1864-1873

I

ONE OF THE MOST important of the "forgotten" judicial leaders is the tall, dignified, imposing, determined Salmon P. Chase. He served as Chief Justice in one the most critical periods in history, during the presidencies of Abraham Lincoln, Andrew Johnson and Ulysses Grant. During his long and prestigious career, he was a member of Lincoln's Cabinet, a U.S. Senator and Governor of Ohio.

Chase preceded Lincoln as the predominant advocate for abolishing slavery, which he regarded as a terrible device used by southern states to control the federal government by threatening to withdraw from the Union if slavery were abolished.

Following his leadership in the Free Soil Party, where he coined the phrase "Free Soil, Free Labor, Free Men," Chase became active in the new Republican Party in which he proclaimed what he called the "slave power conspiracy." In this and similar statements, he became a rival of Lincoln's leadership in the Emancipation movement, going so far as to run against Lincoln for the presidency in 1860.

II

Samuel Chase was born in New Hampshire in January 13, 1808. His father died when he was only ten, leaving his mother a poor woman struggling to raise ten children. Fortunately for Salmon, he was sent at any early age to live with his father's brother, Philander Chase, who was a prosperous Episcopal Bishop in Ohio. The Bishop's influence on the boy was profound. He not only supervised his education but also introduced him to the Episcopal Church—a moderate, non-fundamentalist denomination which would occupy much of his creative energy for all of his adult life.

After attending local schools in Ohio and Vermont, Samuel entered Dartmouth College in New Hampshire where he graduated in 1826 with Phi Beta Kappa honors. Two years later, he was admitted to the bar and began what would become a prosperous career as an attorney.

In 1835, Chase married Katherine Gariss, the first of three wives who died after brief marriages. Shortly thereafter, he married Eliza Anne Smith who died just six years later. He then married, for the last time, Sarah Ludlow, whose death in 1852 ended his marital misfortunes. Chase remained a bachelor for the rest of his life, another two decades.

During the 1830s, '40s and '50s, Chase pursued his highly successful legal career in Ohio. One his notable achievements during this time was the publication of an annotated edition of the Laws of Ohio which would become the authoritative source for both attorneys and judges for many decades.

Also during these years, Chase was involved in a variety of anti-slavery organizations. He was, for example, a leader in the American Sunday School Union, a group engaged in helping slaves who had fled from the South. He was also active in the Semi-Colon Club, a national anti-slavery group involved in many efforts to free slaves and which included such notable figures as Harriet Beecher Stowe among its members.

III

In 1847, attorney Chase argued a case before the Supreme Court. This was *Jones v. Van Zant* which concerned the right of the federal government to aid in the perpetuation of slavery in the southern states. Specifically, the issue in the case involved Congressional legislation which required the return of runaway slaves to their "masters." Chase argued that once a slave escaped to a non-slave State, he became a free person and a citizen of the United States with all the rights of a citizen. To most twenty-first century readers, this will sound exactly right. But we must remember that in 1847 the Civil War, which would resolve the issue in support of Chase's argument, was still many years off. Chase was "ahead of his time." Not surprisingly, he lost the case.

Chase supported Martin Van Buren in the 1848 presidential election. His new Free Soil Party was probably instrumental in securing Van Buren's election. A year later, Salmon was elected to the U. S. Senate from Ohio as a Free Soil candidate. While in the Senate from 1849-1855, he was a champion of African-American rights. He opposed the Missouri Compromise of 1850 which allowed slavery in the new Territories.

During the 1850s, Chase was instrumental in uniting Liberal Democrats with the remnants of the dying Free Soil Party to form the new Republican Party. It was he and not—as often supposed—Lincoln who was the primary founder of this Party. In 1855, Salmon was elected the first Republican Governor of Ohio. In this position, he was especially active in promoting two of the most progressive programs of the day: women's rights and prison reform.

By the late 1850s Chase was clearly the leading Republican political figure in the country and one of the leading opponents of slavery. In 1860, He decided to run for the presidency. Lincoln won the Republican nomination overwhelmingly. Once defeated, Chase offered his support to Lincoln both in the general election and during his presidency.

In 1860, Chase was elected to the U.S. Senate from Ohio. He resigned his seat almost immediately to accept Lincoln's appointment as Secretary of the Treasury. In this post, which he occupied throughout the Civil War, he was instrumental in creating the first national banking system. This helped produce for the first time a unified and stable currency for the country as well as a convenient market for selling national bonds to finance the war. He was also responsible for placing the words, "In God we Trust" on all U. S. coins. To honor Salmon for his highly significant accomplishments as Secretary of the Treasury, his likeness was imprinted on the $10.000 bill from 1928-1946.

Despite his many achievements or, perhaps, because of them there was growing friction with Lincoln. This became clear once Chase's intention to run against Lincoln for the presidency in 1864 became evident.

IV

When Chief Justice Roger Taney died in office in 1864, Lincoln appointed Chase as his replacement—no doubt hoping this would dampen his rival's desire to replace him in the Oval Office. Once on the Court, it became clear that Chase would not follow Taney's leadership as a pro-slavery Chief Justice. Hardly was he settled in office, when he allowed John Rock, the first African-American lawyer ever to do so, to argue cases before the High Court.

Chase's achievements as Chief Justice, though certainly not insignificant, are just as surely not the most important of his accomplishments in public life. In 1868, he presided in the Senate over the impeachment trial of President Andrew Johnson. Johnson was accused of ignoring the authority of Congress to approve or reject his Cabinet appointments by simply designating a Secretary of War on his own authority. Chase ruled that the appointment was invalid because congressional approval for such an appointment was required under the Constitution.

Among a number of Important cases decided by Chase while Chief Justice are: *Texas v. White*(1968), *Veazie v. Banks of Fenno* (1870) and *Hepburn v. Griswold* 1870). In the *Texas* case, Chase ruled that

Confederate States could still be considered a part of the Union for purposes of the application of congressionally approved "Reconstruction Programs" visited upon them and that must obey requirements under that authority. The *Veazie Banks* case ruled that the federal government had the right to tax state bank notes out of existence if it thought this necessary to insure a single national currency.

The *Hepburn* case was an especially complex matter involving congressional power to issue paper money and legal tender notes which had the value of currency. Ruling for the Court, Chase decided that in some cases Congress lacked such authority. This decision seemed so significantly to limit the power of the federal government to regulate the currency that it led directly to a national economic crisis. Within just over a year, the Court reversed Chase's opinion and held that the issuing of legal tender notes by Congress was constitutional.

V

Shortly after these decisions, Chase died, on May 7, 1873, while still serving on the Court as Chief Justice.

Among memorials to his remarkable career in public life are a notable variety of institutions and locations—demonstrating the importance and breadth of his contributions: the Chase National Bank in New York City (now the J. P Morgan-Chase Bank); Chase Hall at the U.S. Coast Guard Academy; Chase County in Kansas; Chase Hall at the Harvard Business School; the Salmon P. Chase College of Law at Northern Kentucky University and The U.S. Coast Guard Cutter, *Chase*.

Morrison Remick Waite

MORRISON WAITE
(1816-1888)
1874-1888

I

T HE SEVENTH SUPREME COURT Chief Justice, Morrison Waite, held that post during one of the most challenging periods in American history. In this post-Lincoln era, the struggle between privates companies, state governments and the federal government for control of the growing economy was at its peak. The resolution of these formative conflicts would define the nature of the American economy and political system for decades to come.

Waite was, by all accounts, a reserved, serious, hard-working and altogether moderate person. Some have seen him as a mediocre leader without personal ambition or serious goals for the country. Others, like one of his successors on the High Court, Chief Justice Harlan Fiske Stone, had a very different opinion. Stone called Waite the greatest Chief Justice after Roger Taney. What is true is that he was a leader with very little political experience before reaching the Court and that he was virtually unknown at that time by the general public.

Probably what is best remembered about Waite is the highly complex and controversial manner in which he became Chief Justice. We will explore this and other aspects of his career in what follows. I think we will come to see that he was one of the most successful and influential Chief Justices in our history.

II

Morrison Waite was born in Lyme, Connecticut in November, 1816. His father, Mason Waite, was a successful attorney who served as Chief Justice of the Connecticut Supreme Court.

A graduate of Yale University in 1837, one of his classmates was Samuel Tilden who would be a U.S. presidential nominee in 1873. Waite was an outstanding student at Yale, graduating with Phi Beta Kappa honors.

In 1840, Morrison moved to Ohio and married his second cousin, Amelia Warner. The couple enjoyed an apparently happy and mutually supportive marriage and had three sons.

The Waites moved to what would prove to be their permanent home in Toledo, Ohio in 1850. Morrison soon became a highly successful attorney--widely respected and admired throughout the state.

III

So well-known and respected was Waite by the time of his marriage that he was comfortable running for a seat in the Ohio Senate. He was easily elected in 1849 and served for one term. This was to be his only elective public office before becoming Chief Justice in 1874!

In 1871, President Ulysses Grant appointed Waite one of three representatives to negotiate a treaty with Great Britain in order to resolve conflicts over the role of that country in supporting the South during the Civil War. At the tribunal called to settle the matter held in Geneva, Switzerland, Waite took a leadership role and was so successful that he won a $15 million settlement from England. Returning home, he was widely celebrated for this achievement and began to gain a national reputation. This was, however, to be the only significant achievement in his public life before becoming Chief Justice.

IV

Waite's nomination to be Chief Justice is the strangest and most complicated such process ever experienced in the long history of appointments to that high office.

In May, 1873, Salmon Chase died while still serving as Chief Justice. In November, President Grant offered the position to Senator Roscoe Conklin of New York who declined to be considered. The post was then offered to Senators Oliver Morton of Indiana and then to Timothy Howe of Virginia, who also turned it down. Next Grant asked his Secretary of State, Hamilton Fish, and then both his Attorney General. George Williams, and former Attorney General, Caleb Cushing, and they declined as well.

Finally, no doubt in desperation, Grant offered the position to the virtually unknown and almost totally inexperienced Morrison Waite, who accepted at once. The choice was not well received anywhere. The journal, *The Nation,* spoke for most in an article on the subject: "Mr. Waite stands in the front rank of second-rate lawyers." Nevertheless, The Senate approved Grant's nomination and Waite assumed the post of Chief Justice in 1874.

As Chief Justice, Waite was unabashed in announcing, almost at once, that his whole life had been a preparation for this office and that he thought himself well-qualified to hold it. During his fourteen years in office, he would preside at the inauguration of no fewer than four U. S. Presidents: Rutherford B. Hayes, John Garfield, Chester Arthur and Grover Cleveland. These men, like himself, are not generally regarded today as among the great figures in American history. But, like him, they served effectively in a very formative if largely forgotten period in our history.

What was central to every issue in those times was the need to resolve major conflicts among the major powers vying for dominance in the country: private business, which was expanding at an unprecedented rate; the federal government, which in the Lincoln era had grown in power; the states, which were striving to assert complete authority, especially regarding economic matters, within their borders.

Waite quickly made it clear that he would try to turn back the growing power of the federal government. His decisions on the Court would reveal this intention by steadily rejecting presidential and congressional regulatory efforts. Neither did Waite approve of what he saw as pretentious efforts of private business to have its way, without what it regarded as "government interference." His many decisions on the Court reflect his strong preference for state government regulation *viz a viz* the power of both the federal government and private business.

One of the first of these decisions, *U. S. v. Cruikshank* (1877), upheld the right of a state to deny voting rights to blacks. Waite argued that the 15th Amendment to the Constitution had granted black citizenship but not voting rights. The two were not the same. States had the right to deny voting rights if they chose to do so. In *Wright v. Nagle* (1879), the Waite Court allowed the State of Georgia to build its own bridges despite "exclusive" rights to do so previously granted to private companies. Similarly, in *Munn v. Illinois* (1877), the power of states to regulate private business was affirmed in a case involving a state setting new rates that might be charged by railroad and grain elevator operators, regardless of previously approved rates.

In 1886, the Waite Court made one of its decisions limiting the power of private enterprise in the face of the authority of a state government. In this case it upheld the right of a state to limit changes which a railroad company might make in its rates despite the fact that the charter (contract) creating the railroad had granted it such rights. (*Stone v. Farmers Loan and Trust Company*).

Rarely, if ever, has there been a Chief Justice who has been so strongly and consistently committed as Waite to the rights of state government both in relation to the federal government and private enterprise.

V

Morrison Waite died suddenly of pneumonia at his home in Toledo, Ohio on March 23, 1888 while still serving as Chief Justice. His death came as a surprise because even those who were close to him had never known him to suffer a serious illness throughout his long life.

Many memorial services were held in his honor at the time but his only significant permanent memorial is the Waite High School in Toledo.

Melville Fuller

MELVILLE FULLER
(1833-1910)
1888-1910

I

T HE "FULLER COURT," AS it was known at the time, was highly
influential in settling major political issues of the late 19th and early
20th centuries involving the relationship between individual rights and
the regulatory authority of government. Melville Fuller, who served as
Chief Justice for more than twenty years during this formative period
in our history, was instrumental in assuring the protection of individual
liberties as the predominant characteristic of the American political
system.

A leading politician from Illinois, Fuller attended almost every
national Democratic Party Convention between 1864 and 1880. He
was, nevertheless, only a minor figure in the country at large until he
reached the Supreme Court in 1888.

Fuller is best remembered today, if at all, for rendering one of the
most controversial and important decisions in the history of the High
Court: *Plessey v. Ferguson* in 1896. This case justified racial segregation
by asserting the "separate but equal" doctrine which affirmed the right
of each state to have its own laws on the subject of segregation. Blacks
may have long ago been granted citizenship and therefore the right to

Philip Secor

vote. But this, argued Fuller did not necessarily grant them other rights such as equal access to public accommodations or other commercial; venues.

II

Melville Fuller was born in Augusta, Maine, on February 11, 1833. His paternal ancestors dated back to the landing of the Pilgrims at Plymouth Rock in 1620. Melville's family had a long history as successful judges and attorneys in New England. Shortly after his birth, his parents divorced and the boy was raised by an uncle who guided him through a good education and into a career in the law.

Graduating from Bowdoin College in 1853, with Phi Beta Kappa honors, Fuller attended Harvard Law School for a time but did not graduate. Even without a degree, he became a well-regarded attorney and was elected to the Augusta Common Council in 1856. Two years later, he married Calista Reynolds. When she died in just seven years, he married Mary Coolbaigh. The couple would have six children—all girls.

In 1860, the Fullers moved to Chicago where he created his own law firm and his career as an attorney flourished. He became active in state politics when he ran the Illinois campaign in Stephen Douglas' unsuccessful bid for the White House against Abraham Lincoln. During these busy years in his career, he also argued several cases before the Supreme Court.

During the Civil War, Fuller avoided military service but was active in Illinois promoting the Union cause. At the same time, however, he was publically critical of most aspects of Lincoln's conduct of the War. Not surprisingly, the two men soon became lasting political enemies.

III

In the decades before he became Chief Justice in 1888, Fuller was a relatively minor figure in American politics. Even in his home State of

Illinois, he did not play a major role, serving but only a single term in the State House of Representatives. His major public activity during these years was his attendance as an Illinois delegate to Democratic Party Conventions in 1864, 1872, 1876 and 1880. His general posture at the conventions was to oppose most of Lincoln's efforts to eliminate slavery, notably the *Emancipation Proclamation* which he vigorously denounced as an unconstitutional expression of federal and especially presidential power. His position was that slavery was a matter for individual states to decide.

Three times President Grover Cleveland offered Fuller positions in his administration, first as Chair of the Civil Service Commission and then as Solicitor General. He turned both offers down. Later, he was offered the post of Secretary of State and said no thanks to that as well. Finally, in 1888, Cleveland offered to nominate him to the Senate as Chief Justice of the Supreme Court and he responded with an enthusiastic "YES."

IV

The Senate response to Cleveland's nomination of Fuller on April 30, 1888 was decidedly unenthusiastic. Many in that body branded him a "traitor" for avoiding military service in the Civil War and later seeking to defeat legislation in the Illinois Legislature to support the war effort. Nevertheless, the Senate, after contentious debate, approved the nomination by a vote of only 41-20.

As Chief Justice, Fuller was usually opposed to the regulatory authority of state governments. However, in his most famous decision, *Plessy v. Ferguson* (1896), he held that segregation was legal if a state allowed it within its borders—one of the most extravagant grants of state power ever allowed by the Court. The Black man might have citizenship and even the right to vote byt these became essentially meaningless under the "separate but equal" doctrine enunciated by Fuller in this decision. As the noted historians, Henry Commager, Samuel Morison and William Leuchtenburg have noted in Volume 1 of their acclaimed *The Growth of the American Republic* (1969):

What all this meant . . .was that the Southern Negro was exiled to a kind of no-man's land halfway between slavery and freedom. He was no longer a slave; he was not yet free. He was excluded from most professions and from many jobs. He was fobbed off not only with segregated schools that were probably inferior, and with "separate" accommodations that were rarely "equal." At first gradually, then with dramatic speed, he was rendered politically impotent: "grandfather clauses," literacy tests, poll taxes, and—where these failed—naked intimidation deprived him of the vote.

In another important case, *Pollock v. Farmers Loan and Trust,* Fuller ruled the federal income tax unconstitutional. In yet another case involving a conflict between a federal law (the Sherman Anti-Trust Act), which prohibited monopolies, and a private corporation, which produced over 90% of all sugar in the country in clear violation of that law, he declared the law inapplicable, allowing the sugar company to continue in operation (*United States v. E. C. Knight Company*-1895).

A final case worth noting during Fuller's twenty-two years as Chief Justice is *Gonzales v. Williams* (1904). This case involved Puerto Rico which became a U. S. Territory after the Spanish American War of 1898. At issue was the right of a Puerto Rican to enter the Unites States in the face of U. S. laws prohibiting them from doing so. Fuller ruled that they had the right to immigrate because these laws were unconstitutional as applied to residents of a U. S. Territory.

V

Melville Fuller, like his predecessor, Morrison Waite, was in office long enough to administer the oath of office to many presidents, in his case five, compared tp Waite's four. They were: Benjamin Harrison, Grover Cleveland, William McKinley, Theodore Roosevelt and Howard Taft. Overall he served twenty-two years as Chief Justice, third in length of service to John Marshall at thirty-four years and Roger Taney at twenty eight years.

In addition to his generally anti-government authority *viz-a-viz* private enterprise legacy as Chief Justice, Fuller is also noteworthy for his strong anti-civil rights stance both regard to both Blacks and Asians.

Melville Fuller died on [GET DATE] in 1910 while still in office. [GET MORE INFORMATION ON LATER YEARS AND DEATH]

Edward White

EDWARD DOUGLAS WHITE
(1845-1921)
1910-1921

I

THERE IS LITTLE DOUBT that one of the least remembered of the seventeen Chief Justices is Edward White, who served during the presidencies of William Howard Taft and Woodrow Wilson. He held only a few other government positions and was not well-known at all outside his native Louisiana.

Not only was White a minor figure in history but what little is remembered about him is generally unfavorable and controversial. As we shall see, both his military service during the Civil War—or lack thereof—and the rationale for his selection as Chief Justice have damaged his reputation.

Historians of the High Court are, however, aware of a few minor items of interest in his life and career such as the facts that he was one of only three Confederate citizens and one of relatively few Roman Catholics ever to serve on the Supreme Court.

The one important contribution of White to the history on both the Court and the nation at large is his enunciation of the "rule of reason" doctrine for deciding cases before the Supreme Court. This "common sense," pragmatic rationale stood in sharp contrast to the more rigid use of "precedent" and literal interpretations of the Constitution as standards for evaluating the legitimacy of laws. As such, it was truly a landmark decision in the history of the Supreme Court.

II

Edward Douglas White was born on November 3, 1845 into a wealthy and staunchly Roman Catholic Louisiana family. His father was a sugar plantation owner who had been Governor of the State and a U. S. Congressman.

Growing up in a family that was very active in the Roman Catholic Church, it is not surprising that William studied at a Jesuit College in New Orleans and later at St. Mary's College in Maryland. Later still, he graduated from George Washington University after a stint at the University of Louisiana (later named Tulane University.)

Before graduating from George Washington University, White PROBABLY enlisted in the Confederate Army. I say "probably" because here is where the most important and controversial episode in his life begins. Did he really see military service as a Confederate lieutenant during the Civil War, as he alleged or, as many later observers have claimed, was this just a manufactured tale designed to enhance his reputation and his hopes for high political office? Stories on both sides of this argument abound. One story is that he was nearly captured by Union forces but escaped by hiding under the hay in and old barn. Another is that he was a hero in conflicts surrounding the great Battle of Vicksburg for control of the Mississippi River in Louisiana in 1863 and also in fighting in the Port Huron area of Michigan, also part of the struggle for the Mississippi. What is certain is that White was imprisoned by Union forces in New Orleans sometime before his release from captivity in 1865.

The reason why these tales of White's supposed Civil War exploits are so important is that they were raised with great fanfare during the nomination debate surrounding his bid for the Chief Justice position in efforts both to support his candidacy and to discredit him. Was he a hero or a liar became the key issue in these often heated discussions.

III

In 1868, after finally receiving his law degree, White opened what would soon become a successful practice as an attorney. By 1879, his reputation was so well established that he was appointed an Associate Justice in the Louisiana Supreme Court and, in 1891, He was elected to the United States Senate.

Just three years later, in 1894, President Grover Cleveland nominated White to be an Associate Justice on the U. S. Supreme Court. In that same year, he married Leita Kent, a widow whom he had been pursuing for nearly twenty years—both before and after her first marriage.

It is noteworthy that, while on the High Court, White voted with the majority in the famous (infamous?) case of *Plessy v. Ferguson* (1896) which allowed racial segregation in states that desired it.

IV

When Chief Justice Melville Fuller died in office in 1910, President William Howard Taft nominated White to as his replacement, despite the fact that he himself was a Republican and White was a Democrat. His reasoning was probably that White, at age 65, wouldn't live much longer and he–Taft—might therefore achieve his own goal which to be Chief Justice after he left the White House. (This, by the way, is exactly what happened, although Taft had to wait a decade for White's demise, probably longer than he had hoped .)

Despite his earlier vote in *Plessy v. Ferguson* in support of racial segregation, once in the Chief Justice chair, White became a strong defender of the rights of African Americans. He especially resisted attempts in some southern states to deny black citizens the right to vote. (*Guinn v, United States,* 1915.)

In another important decision, *Selective Draft Law Cases* (1918,) White upheld the Selective Service Act of 1917 which gave states the right to draft their citizens into military service. Otherwise little of importance was decided by the White court with the major exception of the earlier "rule of reason" decisions highlighted by *Standard Oil of the United States v. The United States* (1911.)

In this landmark decision, the White court held that Standard Oil was in violation of the Sherman Anti-trust law simply because it was "unreasonable" in some of its practices. By implication, therefore, "reasonable" restraint of trade might be allowable. The "rule of reason" standard meant that more fixed ideological use of precedents and strict interpretation of the Constitution might be replaced by a more pragmatic, common-sense look at the specific circumstances in each case.

V

Edward White died while still Chief Justice on May 19, 1921 following a sudden and short illness. Memorials to him are few but do include a statue in the National Statuary Gallery in Washington, D. C. and another statue in front of the Supreme Court building in New Orleans.

Not surprisingly, there is also a Roman Catholic high school in Thibodary, Louisiana named for this life-long and deeply committed church member.

William Howard Taft

WILLIAM HOWARD TAFT
(1857-1930)
1921-1930

I

THE ONLY PERSON EVER to serve as both Chief Justice and President of the United States, William Howard Taft also held many other important positions in the government before he reached the High Court. In all of these posts he was an active and effective performer.

Despite his successful career, Taft was often unpopular with those who worked with and for him as well as with those he served. He was so determined to accomplish his goals that he offended many in the process and was regarded by some at the time as arrogant and overly assertive.

As President, Taft was especially aggressive and, at the same time, very successful in achieving such goals as: the passing of the 16th Amendment to the Constitution which gave Congress the power to levy income taxes; the "dollar diplomacy" with South American countries which extended U. S. economic power in that region; "trust busting" which broke up many monopolies at home; civil service reform; and much more.

In addition, Taft, as we shall see, was a prominent leader in many other government positions including serving as the first civilian

Governor of the Philippines, Solicitor General of the United States and Secretary of War.

II

William Howard Taft was born on September 15, 1857 in the suburbs of Cincinnati, Ohio. He could trace his ancestry to colonial days in Massachusetts. His father, Antonio Taft, was a leading Republican in the country who had served as Secretary of War and Attorney General during the presidency of Ulysses Grant.

In 1878, Taft graduated from Yale University, ranking second in his class. While at Yale, he was a member of the wrestling and debate teams as well as Skull & Crossbones, the secret society formed years earlier by his father when he was a student at Yale.

After college, William attended the University of Connecticut School of Law and was admitted to the Ohio Bar in 1880. Shortly thereafter, he was appointed Assistant Public Prosecutor for Hamilton County, Ohio. Several years later he married his childhood sweetheart, Helen Herron. She would be a profound influence on his career thereafter, always urging him to take positions that she felt would one day lead him to the White House. This very politically active woman tried to prevent her husband's own driving ambition to become Chief Justice of the Supreme Court. Both were to have their way—she when he became President in 1909 and he, when in 1921, he reached his life-long ambition and became Chief Justice.

III

In 1890, at the age of thirty-two, Taft was appointed Solicitor General of the United States by President William Henry Harrison—the youngest person ever to hold that important position. Two years later, he was made a judge on the U. S. Court of Appeals for the Sixth Circuit. While serving on the court, he became the first Dean and Professor of Constitutional Law at the University of Cincinnati.

At the beginning of the twentieth century, Taft had one of the most important political assignments in his career when, in 1900, President William McKinley made him chairman of a commission to form the first civilian government for the Territory of the Philippines. (The Philippines had been ceded to the U. S. by Spain as part of the settlement of the Spanish-American War.) In 1901, Taft accepted appointment as the first Governor of the Territory and served with effectiveness until he felt he had accomplished his goals, despite entreaties by many for him to accept the post he had always desired most--a seat on the Supreme Court.

Taft's determination to complete the work he had begun, which was to establish a stable government in the Philippines, led him to decline an offer from President Theodore Roosevelt to accept appointment as a Justice on the Supreme Court—the one position he had desired since the beginning of his career. No other single act of dedication so clearly demonstrates the unusual determination and dedication of this man—although some would call it just plain "stubbornness."

In 1904, he decided, finally, that his work as Governor of the Philippines was completed and so he accepted an offer from Roosevelt to serve in his cabinet as Secretary of War. In this office, which he held from 1904 to 1908, Taft was the *de facto* Secretary of State, assisting the president in virtually all foreign policy matters. Furthermore, when Roosevelt was out of the country Taft became a virtual "acting president"—so close was the relationship between the two men.

At the time Roosevelt named Taft his Secretary of War, he said to him: "If only there were three of you, I could appoint one of you to the court, one to the War Department and one to the Philippines."

As Secretary of War, Taft was especially active in Japan and Cuba. In Japan, he met personally with Prime Minister Katsawa Taro and formulated an important foreign policy statement which bears his name. In Cuba, he served in 1906 as Civil Governor following the settlement of an internal war which Roosevelt had stopped by sending troops to the Island.

In 1908, Taft's wife, Helen, who was always very much a part of his career in public life, urged him to run for the presidency. In many ways, he was the most obvious choice to run on the Republican ticket as a successor to Roosevelt. His Democratic opponent in the general election was William Jennings Bryan, who had run and lost in two earlier presidential elections. Taft narrowly won the popular vote with only 51% but won by an overwhelming 159 votes in the Electoral College.

At the time of his election as President, Taft was extremely overweight--at over three-hundred pounds--and suffered from sleep apnea. These conditions no doubt contributed to his widely noted argumentative and rigid behavior in public life. He was far less progressive in his policies than Roosevelt had been and had almost none of his predecessor's charm and political savvy. Almost completely unwilling to compromise, much less experiment, he tended to stick closely to a literal interpretation of the Constitution in determining whether a particular action was permissible.

In foreign affairs, Taft was especially cautious in the use of presidential power, usually opting to refer contentious matters to arbitration by various international organizations. Even when anti-Americans riots had broken out in Mexico in 1910 and he had sent troops to the border, he ordered them not to invade Mexico until and unless Congress declared war. Unlike presidents before and after him, Taft did not believe that the constitutionally granted "commander in chief" power gave the president the right to declare an "emergency" and go to war without congressional approval.

In the election of 1912, Taft sought a second term in the White House, running against none other than Roosevelt. (By this time the two had become bitter enemies.) When Taft won the nomination, Roosevelt formed the Progressive Party and ran against him and the Republican candidate, Woodrow Wilson, in the general election. Wilson won handsomely in both the popular and electoral votes. Taft carried only 25% of the popular vote and eight votes in the Electoral College. This was the worst defeat in history for an incumbent president.

After leaving the White House, Taft remained active and prominenet as a writer, lecturer and spokesman supporting many institutions and policies. He became Chancellor of the Yale law School in 1913 and, in the same year, was named President of the American Bar Association. He was also a leading spokesman for the new League of Nations and against laws prohibiting the sale of alcoholic beverages.

IV

Finally, Taft achieved his life-long ambition when, in 1921, the Senate approved President Warren Harding's nomination of him to be Chief Justice of the Supreme Court, shortly after the death of incumbent, Edward White. His "dream come true," as he called it, had come to pass.

Taft's record as Chief Justice is far more noteworthy than his accomplishmrnts as president. He completely reorganized the entire federal judicial system in such a way as to give the Supreme Court more power than ever before. He also saw to the construction of a new Supreme Court building which is still in use. (Previously the Court had shared space with Congress in the crowded Capitol Building.)

While on the Court, Taft delivered more than 250 opinions. He was a decidedly "conservative" Chief Justice, looking usually to historical precedent and the special circumstances of a case rather than the power of Congress or the President for his rationale. His decisions were generally non-ideological and nonpolitical in nature. Among the most important of them were: *Truax v. United States* (1921) which asserted individual rights over power of a State to regulate business; *Bailey v. Drexel Furniture* (1922) declared the Child Labor law of 1919invalid because Congress does not have unlimited taxing power; *Balzac v. Puerto Rico* (1922) which asserted that the Bill of Rights does not apply to overseas territories; *Carrol v. United States* (1925) which decided that, despite the 4th Amendment, which prohibits "unreasonable search and seizure", police may search cars without a warrant if they have "probable cause" to suspect a theft; *Myers v. United States* (1926) said that the President may lawfully remove one of his subordinates without

Senate approval even though that approval had been required for his or her appointment; *Olmstead v. United States* (1928), affirmed that the Supreme Court may exclude evidence in a case which obtained it without a warrant if the case involves telephone wire-tapping, despite the 4th Amendment prohibition of "unreasonable search and seizure."

In general terms, these and Taft's other decisions were not necessarily consistent with one another but did tend to favor a *laissez faire* system in both the government and economy. Not at all doctrinaire in the decisions themselves, he was an absolutist when it came to the Court. Again and again, he affirmed the power of the Court to decide matters involving state and national government exercises of power. The Court would intervene to decide what was allowable and what was not under the Constitution. Taft seemed to regard the Court, and especially the Chief Justice as THE law of the land.

In retirement, when he looked back on his career, he said: "I do not even remember that I was ever President." Clearly, being Chief Justice was the most satisfying part of his long and eventful career in public life.

V

Taft died on March 30, 1930, about a month after leaving the Court. Other Tafts would later rise to high government positions, including his son, Robert, who would be the Republican leader in the Senate and his grandson, Robert, who was also a dominant figure in the Senate as well as one of the most influential Republican leaders in the 1970s and '80s.

His lasting memorials are many, including schools, towns and streets all over the country. Not surprisingly, the William Howard Taft National Historic Site is in his hometown in Ohio and the Ohio Court of Appeals in Cincinnati are named in his honor.

Charles Evans Hughes

CHARLES EVANS HUGHES
(1862-1948)
1930-1941

I

IN SO MANY WAYS, Chief Justice Charles Evans Hughes was similar to his predecessor, William Howard Taft. Both men served for about a decade and both held many high government posts before becoming Chief Justice. More importantly, both were non-ideological, pragmatic decision-makers on the High Court who variously supported and opposed government actions depending on their own strict interpretation of the Constitution as it applied to the particular circumstances of each case. For this apparently inconsistent approach to acts of Congress, the President and state legislatures and governors, Hughes, like Taft before him, was often regarded as an unreliable and even uninformed Chief Justice.

Despite such criticism by some of his contemporaries, most historians have viewed Hughes as one of our best Chief Justices, one of the leading Republicans and greatest attorneys of his day. True, he supported some of President Franklin Roosevelt's "New Deal" programs and declared others unconstitutional. This may have confused and annoyed liberals and conservatives alike but it did not mean that Hughes lacked a consistent basis for his decisions—only that he was a moderate and pragmatic Republican in an era when ideological extremists seemed to dominate both parties.

II

Charles Evans Hughes was born in Glen Falls, New York on April 11, 1862. His father was a Baptist minister who saw to it that his only child was deeply imbued with religious beliefs and did his best to steer him toward a career in the ministry. At age sixteen, in 1874, Charles attended the strongly Baptist, Colgate College (named Madison University at the time), at his father's direction and then transferred to another Baptist school, Brown University, where he was active in many campus activities, earned high grades and received his B.A. degree with Phi Beta Kappa honors in 1882. At this point he entered the law school at Columbia University, earned his degree two years later, in 1884, and began practice in a prestigious New York law firm, where he met his future wife.

In 1888, Charles married Antoinette Carter, the daughter of the owner of the law firm for which he worked and which soon became Carter, Hughes and Cravath. The couple would have four children, a son and three daughters. Shortly after their marriage, Charles suffered a spell of ill-defined "poor health" and withdrew from his law practice. He was hired as a professor of law at the Cornell University School of Law where he remained for two years until his health returned and he resumed his law practice in 1893. This highly successful practice and his accompanying public service in a variety of activities throughout New York soon made Hughes one of the most widely known and successful men in the State.

III

Fellow New Yorker, President Theodore Roosevelt, was not long in recognizing Hughes' popularity with the people and asked him, in 1906, to accept his help in a run for the governorship of the State. Hughes was willing indeed to be Roosevelt's protégé and ran successfully for that post as a liberal Republican. In the general election, he defeated the man who is arguably the most renowned and innovative newspaper publisher in American history, William Randolph Hearst.

As Governor, Hughes supported reform legislation designed to regulate businesses involved in what he regarded as public service areas, notably law enforcement and social welfare. He also promoted laws to limit the financial contributions of private businesses to political candidates and office holders. His other policies as governor included such social reforms as the introduction of an 8-hour work day for factory workers under the age of sixteen, a worker's compensation law requiring employers to pay compensation to injured workers and opposition to a proposed federal income tax.

In 1910, Hughes was nominated by President Taft and approved by the Senate as an Associate Justice of the U. S. Supreme Court. He said at the time that Americans live under a Constitution but that Constitution means only what judges say it means. Therefore they are the true guardians of individual liberties and property rights. While on the Court, he generally favored government regulation of business, especially such vital industries as railroads companies. Furthermore, he held that the federal government, and especially Congress, might invalidate state laws that set rates on interstate commerce, especially commerce by railroads. He nevertheless decided, like Taft before him, that when a state was granted permission to regulate commerce within its own borders, this was permissible under the Constitution. Also, like Taft, he seemed inconsistent in such rulings by his persistent critics.

In 1916, with the encouragement of President Roosevelt, Hughes resigned from the High Court and ran for the presidency. He lost in a close election to Woodrow Wilson, the Governor of New Jersey. Charles then returned to his law practice where he was very successful arguing many cases before the very Supreme Court where he had recently sat as a Justice.

Just a few years later, in March of 1921, the new President, Warren G. Harding, appointed Hughes his Secretary of State. While in this post, he headed a delegation to the Washington Naval Conference on limiting naval power throughout the world. Great Britain, France, Italy, Japan. Belgium, China and the Netherlands all sent representatives to the Conference. Several important agreements were reached, with Hughes having a leading role in each.

Also while Secretary of State Hughes, was instrumental in ending the U. S. military occupation of the Dominican Republic in 1923. Returning to his law practice, he was more successful than ever, once again arguing many cases before the Supreme Court. He was also, for at time in the late 1920's, a judge on the International Court of Justice and a co-founder of the National Conference on Christians and Jews. As though all of this activity were not enough to keep him busy, Hughes was appointed in 1921 by Governor Alfred E. Smith to chair the State Reorganization Commission which finally and completely made the Governor the head of state in New York.

IV

In 1930, Hughes reached the apogee of his career when President Herbert Hoover appointed him Chief Justice of the Supreme Court to replace William Howard Taft who had died only weeks after leaving the High Court. Throughout his tenure as Chief Justice, Hughes was an advocate of civil rights. One of his leading cases, decided shortly after joining the Court, was *Near V. Minnesota* in which he ruled that to restrain the freedom of the press was unconstitutional. The case involved a state law that allowed suppression of a newspaper story which involved a Jewish gangster.

Regarding FDR's New Deal programs, Hughes was sometimes supportive and sometimes not. On some occasions he would join with the two liberal Justices, Louis Brandeis and Harlan Fiske Stone such as in the decision in which the Court allowed a minimum wage law in a given state (*West Coast Hotel v. Parrish,* 1937). On the other hand, he sometimes opposed the "New Deal," most notably when FDR tried to "pack" the Court with six additional judges who would support his programs. Hughes staunchly objected to this plan.

In what was arguably his most famous case as Chief Justice, *National Labor Relations Board v. Jones and Laughlin Steel Corporation* (1937), Hughes upheld the Wagner Labor Act of 1935 that had created the National Labor Relations Board which supported the right of workers to organize into unions and to strike. This was decidedly one of the most pro-labor programs of FDR's "New Deal" and Hughes was in his corner all the way, as he was with a number of the President's "liberal" policies.

V

It is worth noting, by way of a concluding comment on Hughes' career, that he was the author of several important books, written shortly before he became Chief Justice in 1930. These include: *Foreign Relations* (1924), *The Pathway to Peace* (1925), *The Supreme Court of the United States* (1928) and *Pan American Peace Plans* (1929). These works provide helpful insights into all aspects of his career on the Court as well as his other noteworthy accomplishments in public life.

Charles Evans Hughes died in August of 1948 at his home in Osterville, Minnesota. He is buried in the Bronx, New York City. Memorials to his remarkable life include the Charles Evans Hughes House in Washington, D. C., Hughes Hall at Cornell University, a quadrangle at Brown University, public school buildings located as far away as California AND—believe it or not—a mountain range in Antarctica!

Harlan Fiske Stone

HARLAN FISKE STONE
(1872-1946)
1941-1946

I

THE TERMS OF HARLAN Fiske Stone and Fred M. Vinson as Chief Justices took place during the period from 1941-1953. These were the tumultuous latter years of FDR's New Deal and "court-packing" scheme and the more moderate era of Dwight Eisenhower's presidency, incorporating both major civil rights and economic policy actsions of the government.

Although Harlan Fiske Stone served as Chief Justice for less than five years, he was a highly influential Justice on the High Court for sixteen years before becoming Chief Justice. Since these years spanned the most controversial period of FDR's "New Deal" initiatives, Stone was caught up in one of the most formative periods both in the history of the Court and the country.

While on the Supreme Court, Stone was often united in his opinions with two of the most progressive Justices of the period, Louis Brandeis and Benjamin Cordoza, in support of New Deal programs. He became such a favorite of FDR that the President appointed him Chief Justice of the High Court when Charles Evans Hughes retired in 1941.

In all, Stone served as a Justice on the Supreme Court from 1925-1946, with less than five of these as Chief Justice. He held only one other high government position in his entire career, serving as Attorney General for about a year in 1924-25. He was, therefore, a Chief Justice with very limited experience, who had one of the shortest terms as Chief Justice in Supreme Court history.

II

Stone was born in Chesterfield, New Hampshire in 1872. He graduated from Amherst High School and later Amherst College where he earned both his BA and MA degrees. In 1898, he graduated from New York University School of Law and began practice in New York City. The following year he married Agnes Harvey. The couple had two sons.

III

In the busy years just before his marriage, Harlan taught for a short time at Adelphi Academy while still working on his MA degree at Amherst. At Amherst he was a classmate of future President Calvin Coolidge who became his life-long friend. After graduation, from NYU Law School in 1898, he served as Dean of the Law School at Columbia University for eighteen years.

During World War II, Stone was a member of the War Department Board of Inquiry which reviewed requests from "conscientious objectors" who had been denied exemption from military service by their draft boards. He tended to be negative about the appeals, regarding such men as "traitors" and "cowards" who were only trying to avoid armed service in defense of their country.

In 1924, Stone's Amherst classmate, Calvin Coolidge, who was now President of the United States, appointed him U. S. Attorney General. He served in that post for less than a year when he was appointed an Associate Justice on the Supreme Court. He was on the Court during the presidencies of Coolidge, Herbert Hoover and throughout FDR's tenure in the Oval Office. He was a major supporter of Roosevelt's highly controversial programs.

One of Stone's early decisions as an Associate Justice during FDR's administration was *United States v. Caroline Products Company* (1938). In this case, he strongly affirmed the Court's power of judicial review of legislative and executive actions in the areas of civil liberties and the economic practices of large corporations. However, he said, this power is not absolute. Each case needed to be considered separately and on its merits to determine whether the Court had jurisdiction.

In one such case, *U. S. v. Darby Lumber Company* (1941), Stone wrote a decision which reviewed an important law, the Fair Labor Standards Act, and decided that it did indeed fall within the purview of the Court. He declared the law to be "constitutional."

IV

By 1941, Stone was such a favorite of FDR's that when Hughes left his position as Chief Justice, the President appointed Harlan as his replacement. He remained Chief Justice until his death about five years later.

The Stone Court was one of the most divided and contentious in history, not surprisingly as this was the era of controversial "New Deal" legislation, described by many of the day as "socialist" or even "communist."

During his short time as Chief Justice, Stone delivered three especially noteworthy decisions. The first of these was *Ex parte Quirin* (1942) in which he upheld the power of the president to have German civilians living in the United States during the War tried in military courts as Nazis. The second was *International Shoe Company v. Washington* (1945) in which he ruled that, under certain circumstances, State courts may have jurisdiction to try foreign companies doing business in this country.

V

The final case I wish to mention is *Girouard v. United States* (1946) which is worth noting if only because, just after reading aloud his dissent in the courtroom, Stone suffered a stroke and died a few hours later at his home in Washington, D. C. at the age of seventy-three.

Among the few lasting memorials to Stone are honorary degrees which he had received earlier in his life from Amherst College, Yale University, Columbia University and Williams College.

Frederick Moore Vinson

FRED M. VINSON
(1890-1953)
1946-1953

I

FRED VINSON, UNLIKE HIS predecessor, Harlan Stone, held many positions of importance before becoming Chief Justice. He was a member of Congress, Secretary of the Treasury and a member of the U. S. Court of Appeals, among other government posts.

A close friend of Harry Truman, Vinson served as Chief Justice throughout Truman's administration. He rejected offers by both Truman and Eisenhower to run, with their support, for the presidency. While serving as Chief Justice, Vinson, like Stone before him, presided over many decisions in the areas of civil liberties and government efforts to regulate the economy—generally favoring the former and opposing the latter.

II

Born in Louisa, Kentucky in 1880, Fred Vinson was the son of the head jailer in a prison near his home. As a boy, he worked with his father in the jail.

In 1912, Fred graduated from Centre College in Kentucky, where he received his legal education, and was soon a successful attorney in his hometown of Louisa—population about 2500. During World War I, he served in the army before marrying Roberta Dixon in 1924. The couple had two sons.

III

In the year of his marriage, Fred ran for a seat in Congress as a Democrat and was elected. He served in the House for seven of the eight terms between 1924 and 1938, losing only in 1928. While in Congress, he became good friends with future President Harry Truman who was a U. S. Senator at the time. The two advised one another regularly on policy matters and were generally close for the rest of their lives.

In 1937, President Franklin Roosevelt appointed Vinson as a judge on the U. S. Court of Appeals for the district of Columbia. While on this Court, FDR appointed him Chief Judge of the U. S. Emergency Court of Appeals which heard complaints over the application of wartime emergency measures by the President.

Vinson resigned from the Court of Appeals in 1947 to accept appointment as Director of the Office of Economic Stabilization. He had served previously for brief periods as Director of War Mobilization and Reconversion and Director of the Federal Loan Administration. By this time, he was nationally recognized as a leading economic advisor and decision-maker in the federal government.

In 1946, Truman appointed his long-time friend Secretary of the Treasury in his administration. His most important work in this post was the negotiation with Great Britain for repayment of a $3.7 million loan made by that country to the United States—the largest such loan up to that point in our history. While serving as Secretary of Treasury, Vinson supervised the beginnings of the International Bank for Reconstruction and Finance and the International Monetary Fund.

IV

Vinson resigned as Secretary of Treasury in the same year that he assumed the post (1946) in order to accept Truman's appointment of him to serve as Chief Justice of the Supreme Court on the death of Harlan Stone. He held this position until his own death in 1953.

As was the case with his predecessor, Vinson found the Court badly divided, so much so that some of its members would not even talk to the others. One group was led by Hugo Black and the other by Felix Frankfurter. The division among members was as much personal as it was ideological. Vinson's major contribution as Chief Justice was to heal the worst of these conflicts, especially those born of personal antagonisms and jealousies.

In all, Vinson wrote seventy majority opinions and thirteen dissents during his seven years as Chief Justice. Many of these were important cases dealing with civil liberties and the relationship between federal and state governments and the economy. The country at the time was struggling with changes wrought by FDR's "New Deal" and Truman's "Fair Deal" programs.

One of Vinson's most notable opinions was his dissenting argument in the landmark case of *Youngstown Sheet and Tube v. Sawyer* (1952). This case involved judicial review of Truman's seizure of the steel industry during a labor union strike. While the Court invalidated the president's right to exercise such authority without Congressional warrant, Vinson dissented, arguing that in emergency situations the president did have such authority. Once again, he was supporting his close friend in the Oval Office.

Two other especially notable cases before the Vinson Court were *Sweat v. Painter* (1950) and *McLaurin v. Oklahoma State Regents* (1950). In the *Sweat* case, Vinson said that while the "separate but equal" doctrine pronounced in *Plessy v. Ferguson* (1896) which allowed racial segregation when permitted by the federal government, especially in the South, was still applicable, it was so only if the segregated facilities were truly equal. In the *McLaurin* case, Vinson said much the same regarding discriminatory actions by state governments.

V

Fred Vinson, like Harlan Stone before him in so many ways, died under almost identical circumstances, a sudden heart attack while still on the Supreme Court. He is buried in his hometown of Louisa, Kentucky. Memorials to him are few, principally a library building at the University of Kentucky where his personal papers and judicial records are held.

Earl Warren

EARL WARREN
(1891-1974)
1953-1969

I

ONE OF THE MOST important and popular Chief Justices in the history of the Court was Earl Warren who held the position during an especially critical period. Issues involving civil liberties were paramount, including rights of the accused before courts and required prayer in public schools. He was on the Court during all or part of the presidencies of four men: Dwight Eisenhower, John Kennedy, Lyndon Johnson and Richard Nixon. Under his leadership, the Supreme Court became so powerful that it came to be regarded as co-equal in the federal government with both the President and Congress.

Before becoming Chief Justice, Warren was very active in California politics. He served as Attorney General of the State and also as Governor for three terms. After retiring as Chief Justice in 1969, he retained his national standing by serving as Chair of the Warren Commission which investigated the assassination of President Kennedy.

II

Earl Warren was born in Los Angeles, California on March 19, 1891. His father, Mathias Warren was a Norwegian immigrant and his mother, Crystal Hernlund, had emigrated from Sweden. Mathias worked part-time in a railroad repair shop in Bakersfield, California and was tragically murdered in 1894 while Earl was still a small boy.

In 1912, Earl earned his BA degree from the University of California, Berkley. He was admitted to the bar in 1914 and practiced law until 1917. Then he enlisted in the Army where he served as a first lieutenant at Camp Lewis, Washington for about a year before leaving the service to work as Deputy City Attorney in Oakland, California.

In 1925, thirty-four year old Earl married thirty-two year old Nina Palmquist, a Swedish immigrant. The couple had six children. Nina lived to be 100 years old, dying in 1993, two decades after her husband's demise.

III

Between 1925 and 1939, Warren served four terms as District Attorney of Alameda County, California. In this post he was known as being "tough on crime." To his credit were many criminal convictions especially in cases involving corruption in government and efforts to avoid the unpopular prohibition laws of the day. He became so well-known nationally as a crime fighter that he was a natural choice to be named Attorney General of California, a post he assumed in 1938.

As Attorney General, Earl became the main force behind the internment of Japanese civilians during World War II. Years later, when this action became widely regarded as a notorious denial of civil liberties beyond what was necessary even in war time, Warren said that he had been wrong and publicly apologized.

In other respects, Warren was an effective State Attorney General. He was especially notable for completely reorganizing State law enforcement agencies in such a way as to make their operation far more effective in the work of crime prevention as well as the investigation of committed crimes.

Beginning in 1942, Warren finally reached the apogee of his long career in State government when he was elected to the first of three terms as Governor of California. In this role he turned State policies into a miniature version of FDR's "New Deal." Public welfare programs, regulation of the economy, protection of civil liberties, improvements in educational programs, extensive public works projects, including highways, bridges and tunnels were all the order of the day. And, with it all, he was more popular with the electorate than ever before.

In what was widely regarded as a nearly certain victory, Warren ran for the vice-presidency in 1948 on the ticket with Thomas Dewey, Governor of New York, against Democratic Senators Harry Truman and Alben Barkley. (This writer still has a treasured ceramic coaster featuring newspaper headlines from the morning after the election proclaiming "Dewey Defeats Truman;" "Dewey-Warren Ticket Victorious.") But all of this was premature; it was not to be. In a remarkable and almost totally unpredicted upset victory, Harry Truman became President of the United States and Earl Warren's hopes for the #2 spot were dashed.

IV

A "favorite son" presidential candidate from California in 1952, Warren was active at the Republican national Convention that year, especially in supporting efforts to thwart Richard Nixon's bid either to be nominated for the presidency himself or to be the number two man on Eisenhower's ticket. In the event, the Eisenhower-Nixon ticket was elected and Warren and Nixon became political enemies for the rest of their careers.

Once in office, Eisenhower promised Warren a seat on the Supreme Court as soon as one was available, which happened almost immediately when Chief Justice Vinson died in 1953. Eisenhower probably chose Warren because he saw in him a somewhat more "liberal" Republican than himself who might broaden the base of his own support in the Party. At the time he said that Warren "represents the kind of political, economic and social thinking that I believe we need on the Supreme Court. . . . He has a national name for the integrity, uprightness and courage we need on the Court." Just a few years later, after Warren's decisions proved to be much too progressive for Eisenhower's taste, he changed his tune dramatically and called his appointment of Warren "the biggest damned-fool mistake I ever made."

Indeed, Warren was to become one of the most progressive Chief Justices in history. Along with Hugo Black and William O. Douglas, he favored using the power of the Court to promote vigorously individual rights over corporate property rights. The other principal group on the Court at the time, led by Felix Frankfurter and Robert Jackson, favored judicial restraint so that Congress and the President might make public policy largely unfettered by Court "interference." Before long, Warren was a chief target of political conservatives throughout the country.

For his part, Warren became something of a "darling" among liberals and a public figure with enormous popularity among most of the general public. Though never a really good legal scholar or cogent opinion writer—his logic often seemed muddled—his decisions were formative for the future direction of the country in many important areas.

For example, one of his truly formative decisions, made shortly after he became Chief Justice, was the landmark case of *Brown v. Board of Education* (1954) which declared racial segregation in public schools to be unconstitutional. This case overrode *Plessey v. Ferguson* (1896) in which the High Court allowed segregation in such public places as schools under the doctrine of "separate but equal." This decision, as we have seen, perpetuated segregation in the South long after the conclusion of the Civil War.

Two of Warren's other important decisions were *Baker v. Carr* (1962) and *Reynolds v. Sims* (1964). The former ended disproportionate representation of rural and suburban areas in state legislatures thereby providing a more accurate representation of minorities. The *Reynolds* case affirmed that if a person was a citizen he was a voter regardless of where he lived. The states complied by apportioning their legislatures so as to allow a fair representation for less wealthy citizens including minorities.

Gideon v. Wainwright (1963) further enhanced the rights of poor people when Warren declared that economically deprived defendants in criminal cases should receive publicly funded attorneys.

One of Warren's most controversial decisions was *Engel v. Vitale* (1962) in which the Court outlawed prayer in public schools. This created a national uproar from many religious groups. Large signs appeared throughout the country proclaiming: "Impeach Warren." Warren's point, however, was that the First Amendment clearly prohibited any law "respecting an establishment of religion."

Continuing his long record of protecting individual rights, Warren said, in *Griswold v. Connecticut* (1963), that there was a constitutional right to privacy which might not willfully be disregarded by any branch of government.

V

Warren retired from the Supreme Court in 1969 at the age of seventy-eight. However, the career of this remarkable man was not yet finished. Reluctantly, he accepted President Lyndon Johnson's appointment to head what was known as the "Warren Commission," charged with investigating the assassination of President John F. Kennedy.

Despite criticism from many then and now, to the affect that the Commission's conclusion ignored too many facts and was too simplistic to be valid, Warren found that a single man named Lee Harvey Oswald, acting on his own initiative and without assistance, had murdered the president. Because the Commission refused to release materials leading to its conclusion, those who disagreed with it elaborated many other theories, some of which involved international conspiracies involving foreign countries.

Earl Warren died on July 9, 1774 at his home in Washington D.C. His funeral service was held at the Washington National Cathedral and he is buried in Arlington Cemetery in the Nation's Capitol. Colleges, schools, streets, fairgrounds and other public places are named in honor of this incredible man in many parts of the country, but mostly in his native State of California. He was awarded the Presidential Medal of Freedom posthumously in 1981.

Warren Burger

WARREN BURGER
(1907-1995)
1969-1986

I

M ANY IMPORTANT DECISIONS WERE made during the term of Chief Justice Warren Burger. Compared with his predecessor, Earl Warren, with his decidedly progressive outlook, this was a period of non-ideological decisions—some liberal and some conservative.

A "strict constructionist," Burger was opposed to government acts which seemed to him not specifically allowed by the Constitution, especially in cases involving executive and legislative acts supporting such "civil liberties" as abortion, school desegregation and gay rights.

Not surprisingly, Burger was a favorite of President Richard Nixon who held similarly mixed, but usually conservative, views on many issues and had appointed Burger to the Court for this reason. Nixon also hoped that Burger would succeed him as president and tried hard to achieve that objective.

II

Warren Burger was born in St. Paul, Minnesota, on September 17, 1907. His parents were farmers living on the outskirts of the city. In high school he was active in sports and student government. In 1937, he graduated, *cum laude,* from the William Mitchell School of Law, known at the time as the St. Paul College of Law. He remained at William Mitchell after he received his degree as a professor for about twelve years.

In 1933, Warren married Elvera Stromberg. The couple had two children, a boy and a girl.

III

In the years before he was on the Supreme Court, Burger was an active Republican Party figure in Minnesota. As such, he vigorously supported Harold Stassen's unsuccessful run for the presidency in 1948 and in 1952 delivered the State's electoral vote to Dwight Eisenhower. As a reward, Ike appointed him Assistant Attorney General in the U. S. Department of Justice.

A few years later, in 1956, Eisenhower appointed Warren a Judge on the U. S. Court of Appeals for the District of Columbia, an important post he held for thirteen years.

In 1969, immediately following Earl Warren's retirement as Chief Justice, Burger's long-time friend and supporter, Richard Nixon—now President Nixon—recommended him to the Senate to be the new Chief Justice. The Senate approved the nomination.

IV

Leading political conservatives throughout the country who, like Nixon, had looked forward to a Chief Justice who would be different from the progressive Earl Warren, were quickly disappointed with Burger who demonstrated that he had mixed views on the conservative-liberal scale.

In one of his early decisions, *Swarm v. Charlotte Mecklenburg Board of Education* (1971), for example, he ruled in favor of busing minority students to predominantly white school in order to reduce the number of segregated schools. Just two years later, in the landmark case of *Roe v. Wade* (1973), he was with the Court majority in supporting women's right to abortion by overruling laws that prohibited it.

In a number of other cases, however, Burger took a much more conservative stand. A good example is one of his last decisions on the Court, *Bowers v. Hardwick* (1986) in which his Court upheld a state law which criminalized such homosexual activity as sodomy.

In general, Burger's performance as Chief Justice was not only ideologically inconsistent regards the content of decisions but also what was often seen as lacking in knowledge of the law. Also, he made little effort to show the sort of leadership on the Court which was generally expected and had been demonstrated by most of his predecessor Chief Justices. An exception was his commendable effort to reform the general structure and administration of the national court system.

Two close students of the Court, Robert Woodward and Scott Armstrong, in their 1979 book, The Bretheren: Inside the Supreme Court, called Burger notably weak and uninformed. One of their sources, Justice Potter Stewart, is quoted as saying that Burger "repeatedly irked his colleagues by changing his notes to remain with the majority." In *Time* magazine, an article at the time described Burger's performance as Chief Justice as "plodding," "standoffish," "pompous," "aloof," and "unpopular."

V

In September, 1986, Burger retired from the Court. He worked for a time on the committee planning the bicentennial celebration of the U. S. Constitution. In 1988, he was awarded the Presidential Medal of Freedom, just as his predecessor Earl Warren, had some years earlier.

At the age of eighty-seven, on June 25, 1995, Burger died at his home in Washington, D. C. He is buried in the Arlington National Cemetery.

There are a few notable memorials to Warren Burger. These include awards from Princeton University and the Academy at West Point received during his retirement years, a courthouse in his native St. Paul and a library at William Mitchell College, both named posthumously in his honor.

William Rehnquist

WILLIAM REHNQUIST
(1924-2005)
1986-2005

I

CONSERVATIVE REPUBLICAN LEADERS, WHO had been at least somewhat pleased with Warren Burger's record of usually opposing both government regulation of the economy and civil rights legislation, had every reason to be delighted when William Rehnquist became Chief Justice in 1986. The new Chief Justice would soon demonstrate a record of decisions that would rank him among the most conservative occupants of that high office in history. He consistently supported states' rights over federal power and asserted the duty of the Supreme Court to strike down acts it regarded as contrary to a strict reading of the Constitution.

That Rehnquist presided over a conservative High Court is not surprising given that this era in American history has been generally regarded as a time of conservative Republican Party dominance. During his years as Chief Justice, the occupants of the White House included Ronald Reagan, George Bush, George W. Bush and the moderate Democrat, William Clinton.

II

William Rehnquist was born in Milwaukee, Wisconsin on October 1, 1924. His father, William, was a paper salesman and his mother, Margery, a homemaker. After graduating from a local high school in 1942, he entered Kenyon College in Gambier Ohio, remaining only a short time before enlisting in the Army Air Force where he served in various posts around the country as a meteorologist. When the war ended, William entered Stanford University in California and earned his BA and MA degrees in political science and, in 1950, he received another MA degree from Harvard University. While at Stanford, he met and dated Sandra Day O'Connor who would later be his colleague on the Supreme Court.

In 1952, Rehnquist settled in Washington, D. C. to work as a law clerk for Supreme Court Justice, Robert Jackson. When he left this post, after only a year, he wrote an article for *U. S. News & World Report* in which he claimed that law clerks often have a persuasive influence on the decisions of the justices for whom they work. While this may seem a presumptuous claim, he had good reason to make it. While clerking for Jackson, he had written a memo to him opposing government-required school desegregation. He did so during the High Court's deliberations in the landmark case of *Brown v. Board of Education of Topeka.* This was the case which effectively outlawed school segregation. In this memo, which Jackson apparently took seriously and which was to become very influential and widely quoted in the legal community, Rehnquist wrote:

> I realize that it is an unpopular and unhumanitarian position, for which I have been excoriated by "liberal" colleagues, but I think *Plessey v.Ferguson* [the 1896 case which allowed school segregation] was right and should be reaffirmed. . . . To the argument . . . that a majority may not deprive a minority of a constitutional right, the answer must be that, while this is sound in theory, in the long run it is a majority who will determine what the constitutional rights of the minority are.

Apart from the clear support of school segregation in this statement, even more revealing is Rehnquist's preference for practical as opposed to ideological reasoning. Never mind, he seems to say, that segregation is morally wrong. In the real world it is always the majority which decides what, if anything will be the rights of the minority. If there was any doubt about his views in this regard, he spoke even more specifically in a later memo to Justice Jackson concerning another case before the Court in which he said:

> The Constitution does not prevent the majority from binding together, nor does it attaint success in the effort. It is about time the Court faced the fact that the people of the South do not like the colored people: the Constitution restrains them from effecting this dislike through State action but it most assuredly did not appoint the Court as a sociological watchdog to rear up every time private discrimination raises its ugly head.

Once again, discrimination is wrong but that is not reason enough to engage action by the Supreme Court. The Court should simply stay out of such matters.

While still clerking for Justice Jackson, Rehnquist married Natalie Cornell in 1953. The couple had three children and moved to Phoenix, Arizona shortly after marriage. William was soon very successful in his law practice in the city. Natalie lived until 1991, some years after her husband became Chief Justice. She died of ovarian cancer.

Very active as a Republican in state politics, Rehnquist campaigned actively in 1964 in the presidential campaign of Barry Goldwater. A few years later, he returned to Washington, D. C. when President Richard Nixon appointed him Assistant Attorney General to John Mitchell.

When Justices Hugo Black and Marshall Harlan resigned from the Supreme Court in 1971, Nixon replaced Harlan with Rehnquist. Before long, he was recognized as the most conservative member of the Court. He almost always favored states' rights over federal power, was skeptical about the Fourteenth Amendment protections of civil liberties and usually supportive of private business over individual property rights. In the 1977 case of *National League of Cities v. Usery,* for example, he was with the Court majority when it struck down a federal law which would have required states to offer minimum wages and maximum work hours. However In many similar cases he supported state laws which mandated such rights.

In all respects, Rehnquist was a "strict constructionist," arguing that it was not the Court's business to apply the changing values of society to current issues. In abortion rights cases, like *Trimble v. Jordon,* he wrote the Court opinion which held that it was irrelevant that social attitudes toward abortion had changed radically since the late eighteenth century when the Constitution was written. He also joined the majority in the Court in the leading case of *Roe v. Wade* (1973) which was definitive in its determination that the Supreme Court had no jurisdiction whatsoever in abortion cases.

For all his years on the High Court—and never more so than when he was Chief Justice—Rehnquist had good relations with his colleagues and was regarded even by some liberals, who clearly disliked his opinions, as a "team player," "good natured," "likeable." A few liberals were not so kind, however. Thurgood Marshall accused him of "misrepresenting facts" and others called him guilty of "misstatements," and "twisting the facts."

IV

In 1986, President Ronald Reagan appointed Rehnquist Chief Justice of the Supreme Court when Warren Burger retired. In this post he was not quite so conservative as he had been earlier, though he still deserves to be regarded as one of the most conservative Chief Justices in history.

His most famous (infamous?) case as Chief Justice is *Bush v. Gore* (2000) in which he wrote a concurring opinion to the effect that there could be no recount of the Florida vote in the presidential election, thereby giving the election to George W. Bush. This was despite an early ruling to the contrary by the Florida Supreme Court. In fact, Al Gore had won the recount vote which, if allowed, would have made him and not Bush the forty-third President of the United States.

In other cases, Rehnquist was somewhat more assertive of the power of the Supreme Court than he had been as an Associate Justice. In *City of Boerner v. Flores* (1997), for instance, he ruled that Congress should defer to the High Court in cases involving the "equal protection of the laws" of the Fourteenth Amendment. Similarly, in *U. S. v. Morrison* (2000), he wrote the opinion which struck down a law giving women civil damages in cases involving physical violence against them. He did so on the grounds that, regardless of current social norms, such actions fall outside what was the original intent of the Constitution.

In an earlier case, *Romer v. Evan* (1996), Rehnquist dissented in a decision which affirmed rights to homosexuals to be protected from discrimination, arguing that they had been given no such rights in the Constitution. He also continued to favor a very restricted application by the Court of the "freedom of speech" provisions in the founding Document. In *Bigelow v. Commonwealth of Virginia,* for example, he opposed any advertising in the public media of abortion or birth control devices as expressions of constitutionally protected "freedom of the press."

V

Long before he became Chief Justice, Rehnquist suffered declining health. As early as the 1970's, he was taking strong medicine for insomnia and severe back pain. Before long he was slurring his words— even while serving on the High Court.

In 2004, Rehnquist was diagnosed as suffering from thyroid cancer and began missing sessions of the Supreme Court altogether. He died on September 3, 2005, just short of his eighty-first birthday and is buried near his home in Arlington, Virginia.

John Roberts

JOHN ROBERTS
(1955-)
2005-

I

ALTHOUGH IT MAY SEEM somewhat presumptuous to write a biography—even a short one—of a sitting Chief Justice, this writer has decided to do so in order to bring this work up to date at the time of publication. Care will be taken, however, not to preclude the possibility that John Roberts, still in his early years on the Court, may change his general judicial outlook before he leaves office.

To date, it is fair to characterize Roberts as quite consistently "conservative" in his decisions. despite the fact that the Court as a whole has demonstrated a "mixed" record on the conservative-liberal scale. The Court has been evenly divided—one group tending to favor individual economic and civil rights as over against the authority of government and power of big business. This group of liberal Justices includes all three women on the Court—Sonia Sotomayer, Ruth Bader Ginsburg and Elene Kagan, along with Stephen Beyer. The conservatives, generally opposing the individual liberties of employees, consumers and small business which are seen as thwarting the interests of big business, are Samuel Alito, Jr., Clarence Thomas, Antonin Scalia and Chief Justice Roberts.

This four-to-four split on the Court would immobilize it were it not for the single "swing" member, Justice Anthony Kennedy who votes sometimes with the conservative group and sometimes the liberals.

The most consistently conservative member of the Court has been Chief Justice Roberts—nearly 100% pro big business.

II

John Roberts was born in Buffalo, N. Y. on January 27, 1955. His father, Robert, was a plant manager for Bethlehem Steel Corporation and his mother, Rosemary, a home-maker. John had three sisters. While still a boy, the family moved to Long Beach, Indiana where he attended a Roman Catholic boarding school and made a record as both an outstanding athlete and excellent student.

In 1976, John graduated, *summa cum laude,* from Harvard College in only three years. He then entered the Harvard Law School where he was editor of the law review and graduated *magna cum laude* in 1979.

Roberts remained single for nearly two decades while pursuing a successful career as a private attorney. In 1996, he married fellow Roman Catholic, Jane Sullivan. The couple has two adopted children, a boy and a girl.

III

In 1980, just out of law school, Roberts became a clerk for Supreme Court Justice, William Rehnquist. Within about a year, President Ronald Reagan appointed him Special Assistant to the Attorney General and a year later, in 1982, he became Associate Counsel at the Reagan White House, serving under Chief Counsel, Fred Fielding.

Four years later, Roberts left government service and returned to private law practice, this time in Washington, D. C. In 1989, he returned to government work as Principal Deputy Solicitor General under Solicitor General, Ken Starr, in the administration of President George H. W. Bush. In 1992, he left government once again to resume his private practice. For over a decade he argued some thirty cases before the Supreme Court, winning twenty-five of them.

The second Bush President, George W. appointed Roberts to serve on the District Court for the District of Columbia. On the court, he consistently voted, as he had in the past, against individual rights claimed in opposition to the authority of government, especially state government. Soon he became famous as a support of States' rights in general. He has also been a *stare decisis* Justice, strongly influenced by previous Court decisions on a similar subject. Sometimes, of course, these two principles are in conflict and when they are, he tends to abandon reliance on precedent in favor of a pro-business position.

IV

When Chief Justice Rehnquist died in 2005, President Bush nominated Roberts as his replacement. During the nomination hearing in the Senate, he said that he did not think that "an all-encompassing constitutional interpretation is the best way to faithfully construe the Constitution. He continued that it "is not my job to call balls and strikes and not to pitch or bat."

This was a good philosophy to express at a confirmation hearing, where it is important to please a majority. In reality, Roberts became ideologically conservative once confirmed by the Senate as the next Chief Justice. Throughout the hearing he displayed his impressive knowledge of past Supreme Court decisions. Though confirmed, he was opposed by leading Democrats including Richard Durban, Charles Schumer, Joseph Biden and Diane Feinstine, and others who voted "NO!"

One of Robert's early decisions as Chief Justice was *Rumsfeld v. Forum for Academic and Institutional Rights* (2006). In this decision, which Roberts wrote, the Court held that colleges which receive federal money for any purpose must allow military recruiters on the campus.

This was clearly a strong affirmation of government power *viz a viz* private institutions.

In a similar case the following year, *Morse v. Frederick,* Roberts was with the Court majority when it held that college students do not have a right to advocate drug use in public schools regardless of their claimed constitutional right to free speech. Another decision in the same year, *Gonzales v. Carhart,* held that, among many areas in which Congress might regulate human behavior, was the right to outlaw abortions.

More recent decisions limiting the rights of individuals have included *United States v. Windsor* which struck down that part of a federal law which provided welfare benefits for married same-sex couples; *Fisher v. Texas* which upheld the University of Texas' policy of using race as a factor in its admissions practices; *Clapper v. Amnesty International* which held against human rights groups, attorneys, political leaders and others who challenged a government surveillance program and *Maryland v. King* which ruled that police have a right to take DNA samples from unwilling arrestees.

One of the most important among recent decisions of the Roberts' Court is *American Express v. Italian Colons Restaurant* (2013) in which the Court held that companies can avoid class-action suits against their actions by including "arbitration clauses" in their contracts with individuals and institutions likely to sue them. Such clauses, the Court held, make mandatory an effort to arbitrate differences rather than take them to Court.

Again, one must be clear that these are the conservative decisions by one-half of the Court which includes Justices Alito, Scalia, Thomas and Chief Justice Roberts. They do not reflect the tenor of the Court as a whole. There have also been important liberal decisions coming from the other half of the Court: Sotomayer, Ginsburg, Kagan and Beyer, with Kennedy making a majority possible by moving from one camp to the other—an exaggeration, to be sure, but generally the case.

V

As mentioned at the outset, Chief Justice Roberts is still on the Court and likely to remain so for many years. Thus, it is not fair to make any final assessment of his record. All that has been attempted here is a brief look at his record thus far, along with a description of his life and career before becoming Chief Justice.

POSTSCRIPT

HAVING COMPLETED THIS SURVEY of the lives and careers of the Chief Justices, it is tempting to look for some similarities among them that might define a general pattern in membership and decisions of the Supreme Court since its founding in 1789.

What we have discovered, I think, both satisfies and disappoints this hope. In a number of respects the Chief Justices have been remarkably similar and in some ways very different. Important similarities include the fact that fourteen of the seventeen graduated from the finest American colleges and universities, including Harvard, Yale, Princeton, Dartmouth, Columbia and Colgate. Most graduated with academic honors and membership in Phi Beta Kappa.

Another pattern is that all seventeen Chief Justices were married and twelve of them had children. Also noteworthy is the fact that most of them were not deeply religious, probably holding what would be regarded as a Deist or Unitarian faith which, while admitting to the likelihood of a spiritual Being who was God as the "Creator" of all life, was more skeptical about such verities as the "virgin birth" or a Savior who was literally "resurrected" from death, "ascended" to heaven and is physically "present" in the Sacraments.

Despite such quiet skepticism among themselves, Justices have been careful not openly to reject religious "truths." They were well aware that to do so could spell defeat for anyone seeking public office. This was, after all, a people whose very existence as a democratic society presupposed the existence and real presence of a God who was simultaneously present and far away.

(It is worth noting that only four of the seventeen Chief Justices in our history have been openly and deeply religious: two Roman Catholics, one Episcopalian and one Baptist. None of these four was an ordained priest or minister. All were laymen.)

Other important similarities among the Chief Justices include the fact that almost all had careers as successful attorneys and political leaders in their States and most had argued cases before the Supreme Court before sitting on the High Court themselves. Finally, one notes that all but three of the seventeen openly described becoming Chief Justice as his highest professional goal years before attaining the apogee of his career. The remaining three, who were just as clear about their dislike of the position—both before and after holding it—were John Jay, John Rutledge and Warren Burger.

Areas of behavior among the Chief Justices which reveal lack of general agreement and similarity include a sharp ideological divide between conservatives and liberals. As we have noted, of the seventeen Chief Justices nine have been generally regarded as conservative and the balance either liberal or moderate "swing voters" on Court cases.

There is also a difference in the family backgrounds of the Chief Justices. Seven grew up in prosperous families, often with fathers who were attorneys and/or high government posts. Some had distinguished ancestors dating back to colonial America. However, a similar number came from modest working-class backgrounds and a few from clearly economically disadvantaged environments.

Finally, there is a nearly even difference in the number who had careers after leaving the Court (9) and those who died while still serving as Chief Justice (8).

In summary, we may conclude that the Chief Justices as a group: 1) have been well-educated and intelligent; 2) enjoyed careers as successful and prominent attorneys; 3) held high office in government before joining the Court; 4) been predominantly conservative ideologically; 5) has not been openly religious; (6 has viewed the Chief Justice position as their career apogee and liked the job once in it.

BIBLIOGRAPHY

GENERAL

Cushman, Clare, *The Supreme Court Justices: Illustrated Biographies,* 2001.

Urofsky, Melvin, *The Supreme Court: A Biographical Dictionary,* 1919.

Finkleman, Paul and Melvin Urofsky, *Landmark Decisions of the United States Supreme Court, 2nd ed., 2008.*

JAY

Casta, William, *The supreme Court in the Early Republic: The Chief Justiceships of John Jay and Oliver Ellsworth,* 1995.

Monaghen, Frank, *John Jay Defender of Liberty,* 1972.

Pafford, John, *John Jay The Forgotten Founder,* 2009.

RUTLEDGE

Barry, Richard, *Mr. Rutledge of South Carolina,* 1993.

ELLSWORTH

Brown, William, *The Life of Oliver Ellsworth,* 1905.

MARSHALL

Newmyer, Kent, *John Marshall and the Heroic age of the Supreme Court,* 2001.

Smith, Jean, *John Marshall, Defender of a Nation,* 1996.

TANEY

Lewis, Walker, *Without Fear of Favor: A Biography of Chief Justice Roger Brooke Taney,* 1965.

Huebner, Timothy, *The Taney Court: Rulings and Legacy,* 2003.

CHASE

Niven, John, *The Salmon P. Chase Papers,* 1993.

Warden Robert, *An Account of the Private Life and Public Services of Salmon Portland Chase,* 1874.

WAITE

McGrath, Peter, *Morrison R. Waite: The Triumph of Character,* 1963.

FULLER

Ely, James, *The Chief Justiceship of Melville W. Fuller, 1888-1910,* 1995.

Furer, Howard, ed., *The Fuller Court, 1888-1910,* 1986.

WHITE

Highsaw, David, *Edward Douglas White Defender of the Conservative Faith,* 1981.

Pratt, Walter, *The Supreme Court Under Edward Douglas White 1910-1921*, 1999.

TAFT

Burton, David, *Taft, Holmes and the 1920s Court: An Appraisal*, 1998.

Lurie, Jonathan, *William Howard Taft: Progressive Conservative*, 2011.

HUGHES

Simon, James, *FDR and Chief Justice Hughes: The Epic Battle Over the New Deal*, 2012.

Pusey, Merlo, *Charles Evans Hughes*, 2 vols., 1951.

STONE

Mason, Alpheus T., *Harlan Fiske Stone: Pillar of the Law*, 1956.

VINSON

St. Clair, James and Linda Gugan, *Chief Justice Fred Vinson of Kentucky: A Political Biography*, 2002.

Urofsky, Melvin, *Division and Discord: The Supreme Court Under Stone and Vinson*, 1997.

WARREN

Newton, Jim, *Justice for All: Earl Warren and the Nation He Made*, 2007.

White Edward, *Earl Warren: A Public Life*, 2007.

Scheiber, Harry, *Earl Warren and the Warren Court*, 2006.

BURGER

Schwartz, Bernard, ed., *The Burger Court: Counter Revolution or Confirmation?* 1998.

Blasic, Vincent, *The Burger Court: The Counter Revolution That Wasn't,* 1983.

REHNQUIST

Hudson, David, *The Rehnquist Court: Understanding Its Impact and Legacy,* 2006.

Schwartz, Herman, *The Rehnquist Court: Judicial Activism on the Right,* 2003.

ROBERTS

McElroy, Lisa, *John G. Roberts, Jr.: Chief Justice,* 2007.

Neubaurer, Davis and Stephen Meinhold, *Battle Supreme: The Confirmation of Justice John Roberts and the Future of the Supreme Court.*